SpringerBriefs in Economics

More information about this series at http://www.springer.com/series/8876

Niklas Elert · Magnus Henrekson
Mikael Stenkula

Institutional Reform for Innovation and Entrepreneurship

An Agenda for Europe

Niklas Elert
Research Institute of Industrial Economics
Stockholm
Sweden

Mikael Stenkula
Research Institute of Industrial Economics
Stockholm
Sweden

Magnus Henrekson
Research Institute of Industrial Economics
Stockholm
Sweden

ISSN 2191-5504   ISSN 2191-5512   (electronic)
SpringerBriefs in Economics
ISBN 978-3-319-55091-6   ISBN 978-3-319-55092-3   (eBook)
DOI 10.1007/978-3-319-55092-3

Library of Congress Control Number: 2017933437

Printed on acid-free paper

This Springer imprint is published by Springer Nature
The registered company is Springer International Publishing AG
The registered company address is: Gewerbestrasse 11, 6330 Cham, Switzerland

Acknowledgements

We thank Mark Sanders and Michael Fritsch for useful comments and suggestions, and Charlotta Olofsson for skillful research assistance.

This study was written as part of the project Financial and Institutional Reforms for an Entrepreneurial Society (FIRES) that has received funding from the EU's Horizon 2020 research and innovation programme under grant agreement No. 649378. We also gratefully acknowledge financial support from the Jan Wallander and Tom Hedelius Foundation, from the Marianne and Marcus Wallenberg Foundation and from Stiftelsen Millenium.

Contents

Executive Summary

The European Union suffers from an innovation deficit, which must be remedied if the EU is to improve the quality of life of its citizens and remain competitive in the global marketplace. In order to do so, more productive entrepreneurship is required. We analyze how Europe's institutional framework conditions could become more supportive of entrepreneurship and innovation, and outline a reform strategy to achieve this objective. To be viable, the strategy emphasizes the large cross-country differences across the union. Each EU member state has evolved its particular bundle of institutions, many of which are complementary to one another. If these complexities are not acknowledged, well-intended reforms may become unpredictable or even detrimental to entrepreneurship and economic development.

Chapter 2 provides a theoretical foundation to help identify the areas where the need for reform is the greatest. The theories of the experimentally organized economy and of entrepreneurial ecosystems are used to identify six competencies, in addition to that of the entrepreneur, that are necessary for ideas to be generated, identified, selected, and commercialized. The competencies are those of inventors, professional managers, competent employees, venture capitalists, actors in secondary markets, and demanding customers. Importantly, no one is in charge of the ecosystem's skill structure, which limits what can be achieved through top-down reform. We also draw on the varieties of capitalism literature, which identifies institutional complementarities as an important driver of the persistent institutional differences across polities. The existence of institutional complementarities implies that viable policy changes must be compatible with existing institutional patterns and that a specific change will have effects that extend throughout the institutional system. As such, they help explain both gridlocks and cascading changes.

In Chap. 3, we discuss the institutions that the previous literature identifies as the most relevant for nurturing the activities of entrepreneurs and other actors in the ecosystem's skill structure. Overall, we discuss nine areas: (i) the rule of law and the protection of property rights; (ii) the tax system; (iii) regulations governing savings, capital and finance; (iv) the organization of labor markets and social insurance systems; (v) regulations governing goods and service markets; (vi) regulations governing bankruptcy and insolvency; (vii) R&D, commercialization and knowledge spillovers; (viii) human capital investments; and (ix) informal institutions. Although our starting point is that some institutions or institutional forms are simply the most propitious for entrepreneurship and economic growth, we complement this first-best perspective with insights offered by the perspectives discussed in Chap. 2, and clarify the extent to which policies and institutions interact with and reinforce one another.

In the fourth and final chapter we summarize the study and present our main conclusions. To make the European Union more entrepreneurial to promote innovation and economic growth we propose a reform strategy with respect to the aforementioned nine areas, which we consider to be the most pertinent institutions and policies in order to foster a productive entrepreneurial economy. Overall, the proposed institutional changes move in a liberalizing direction, but we acknowledge that one-size-fits-all policy reforms aimed at freer markets will not necessarily be successful. Instead, a successful reform strategy must consider country differences that affect the viability of reform. Nevertheless, policymakers must not lose sight of the long-term goal of institutional liberalization to promote entrepreneurship, innovation, and growth. Hopefully, this work inspires both confidence and humility regarding Europe's innovation future.

Chapter 1
Introduction: Europe's Innovation Emergency

Abstract The European Union suffers from an innovation deficit, which must be remedied if the EU is to improve the quality of life of its citizens and remain competitive in the global marketplace. In order to do so, more productive entrepreneurship is required. We analyze how Europe's institutional framework conditions could become more supportive of entrepreneurship and innovation, and outline a reform strategy to achieve this objective. To be viable, the strategy emphasizes the large cross-country differences across the union. Each EU member state has evolved its particular bundle of institutions, many of which are complementary to one another. If these complexities are not acknowledged, well-intended reforms may become unpredictable or even detrimental to entrepreneurship and economic development.

Keywords Deregulation · Economic growth · Entrepreneurship · European Union · Innovation · Institutional complementarity · Institutional reform · R&D · Varieties of capitalism

In *The Moral Consequences of Economic Growth* from 2005, Harvard professor Benjamin Friedman has a message that seems even more pertinent today than when the book was first published: economic stagnation is harmful for a society's moral and democratic values. Dire economic times and a lack of economic opportunities contribute to political populism of all colors. Friedman's (2005) message is a starting point of this volume, and makes what has been labeled "Europe's Growth Challenge" (Åslund and Djankov 2017) seem even more acute. In what follows, we shall argue that innovation is key to improving the prospects for inclusive and encompassing growth across Europe.

Today, the European Union suffers from an acknowledged lack of innovation. A flagship initiative of the Union's well-known 2020 strategy was the so-called "Innovation Union", launched with a tone of urgency in 2010: "We need to do much better at turning our research into new and better services and products if we

© The Author(s) 2017   1
N. Elert et al., *Institutional Reform for Innovation and Entrepreneurship*,
SpringerBriefs in Economics, DOI 10.1007/978-3-319-55092-3_1

are to remain competitive in the global marketplace and improve the quality of life in Europe. We are facing a situation of 'innovation emergency'" (European Commission 2015).[1] In spite of this urgent tone, little has been accomplished in the intervening years. The Union's own composite innovation index, measured by the European Innovation Scoreboard, has only increased modestly since the strategy was formulated (European Union 2016; see also Fig. A.1 in the Appendix).

Increasing innovation therefore remains an imperative, but the way to achieve it is a larger issue. In our view, the common concept that increased R&D spending is the tool that promotes innovation exposes an overly mechanistic view of how the economy functions. New knowledge and inventions are only the first steps in the innovation and commercialization process, and for increased R&D to translate into economic growth, entrepreneurs must exploit the new knowledge and inventions by introducing new methods of production or new products into the marketplace (Bhidé 2008). Hence, if Europeans are to benefit from innovation and investment in knowledge and capital to the greatest extent possible, their economies must become more entrepreneurial (Acs et al. 2009; Baumol 2010).

At first glance, the means of achieving this goal are clear from an economist's perspective. At least since Baumol (1990), there has been a recognition that entrepreneurship and innovation are shaped by a society's rules of the game—its institutional environment (Aldrich 2011; Estrin et al. 2013). Entrepreneurs and other actors in the so-called entrepreneurial ecosystem or skill structure are crucially dependent on this environment. In this study, we seek to determine how Europe's institutional framework conditions could become more supportive of entrepreneurship and innovation, and outline a reform strategy to achieve this objective.

When political and economic institutions are structured to reward productive entrepreneurial activities (such as starting and expanding firms that provide goods and services that people want) at the expense of non-productive and even destructive activities (such as rent seeking or excessive lobbying), then many researchers argue that more innovation and economic growth will occur, at least in the long run (Mueller and Thomas 2000; Hwang and Powell 2005; Acs et al. 2008; Urbano and Alvarez 2014). Thus, we will focus on economic institutions that have previously been identified as particularly relevant for enabling productive entrepreneurship (Hall and Jones 1999; Béchard and Grégoire 2005; Henrekson and Johansson 2009; Bjørnskov and Foss 2013). In summary, we propose institutional reforms pertaining to nine broad areas:

(i) *The rule of law and protection of property rights.* These are the most fundamental rules of the economic system, and all member states must ensure that they are stable and secure. With regard to intellectual property rights, an important balance must be struck between the interests of investors and the need for knowledge diffusion.

---

[1]See http://ec.europa.eu/research/innovation-union/index_en.cfm?pg=why.

(ii) *Taxation*. Many types of taxes affect entrepreneurial decisions. While tax rates should generally be low or moderate, policy makers should strive for simplicity rather than (targeted) concessions, and for a high degree of tax neutrality across owner categories, sources of finance and different types of economic activities.

(iii) *Savings, capital and finance*. These institutions should be reformed to support increased private wealth formation and the creation of a dynamic venture capital industry, since these are crucial sources of financing, particularly in the early stages of entrepreneurial projects. As a large share of savings in the economy currently goes into pension funds, it would be helpful to allow at least part of these assets to be invested in entrepreneurial firms and not just in real estate, public stock and bonds.

(iv) *Labor markets and social security*. Institutions should facilitate the recruitment of workers with the necessary competencies and reforms should strive to remove onerous labor market regulations. Overly stringent employment regulations may also spur actors in the entrepreneurial ecosystem to devise arrangements that circumvent the regulations, ultimately resulting in the emergence of an underground economy. Furthermore, incentives are best served by government income insurance systems that encourage activation, mobility and risk-taking. Social security institutions should enable the portability of tenure rights and pension plans as well as a full decoupling of health insurance from the current employer, to avoid punishing those individuals who leave tenured employment positions to pursue entrepreneurial projects.

(v) *Regulation of goods and service markets*. Preventing market-leading incumbents from unduly exploiting their dominant market positions is essential. Lowered entry barriers are key to this reform area, as is the opening of those parts of the economy that are almost invariably closed to private production, such as healthcare and schooling. Within a well-designed system of public financing, sizeable private production and contestability should be encouraged.

(vi) *Bankruptcy law and insolvency regulation*. Entrepreneurial failure provides valuable information to other economic actors. Failed ventures must be discontinued so that their resources can be redirected to more productive uses. Bankruptcy law and insolvency regulation should therefore be relatively generous and allow for a "second chance". However, filing for bankruptcy should not be too easy, as that encourages undue exploitation and destructive entrepreneurship, harming creditors and the rest of the community.

(vii) *R&D, commercialization and knowledge spillovers*. R&D spending is only an input; for it to translate into economic growth, entrepreneurs must exploit the inventions and created knowledge by introducing new methods of production or new products into the marketplace. Therefore, instead of focusing on quantitative spending goals and targeted R&D support, policy should more generally make it easier to start and grow businesses.

(viii) *Incentives for human capital investment.* Policy should strive to create positive incentives for the individual to acquire knowledge and skills, whether through formal or workplace education. Incentives must also be developed by the education system itself to supply such opportunities. In this respect, the U.S. university system seems more responsive to the economic needs of society than European university systems. The U.S. system could be an important role model, as long as due attention is paid to European concerns regarding accessibility and equity.

(ix) *Informal institutions.* Informal institutions affect the workings of formal institutions but may also be important in their own right for fostering entrepreneurship. Norms and habits that facilitate cooperation and impersonal exchange must be strengthened, particularly with regard to trust. High-trust environments have been found to nurture market entry, enterprise growth and productive entrepreneurship. The extent to which policy can influence this development is nevertheless doubtful.

As our summary of the results suggests, our overall message is that policymakers in member states and at the centralized EU level should institute entrepreneurship-friendly institutions largely by undertaking economic policy liberalization. Ultimately, that was the original intent of much of the European Union project and the promotion of the so-called four freedoms of its single market (of goods, workers, services and capital). Convincing arguments have also been put forth that the Union's procedural logic will inherently push the institutional setups of member states in a liberalizing direction (Scharpf 2010).[2] However, the manner in which countries undertake reforms is fundamentally important.

A best-practice reform approach would be to identify a country (whether a member or non-member) that appears to be performing well in a particular institutional dimension and to promote and adopt this institution in other countries (Rodrik 2008). Indeed, this type of approach has been extensively promoted by organizations such as the World Bank and the IMF, especially in developing countries. This is problematic for several reasons.

First, first-order economic principles—such as the protection of property and contract enforcement—do not map onto unique policy packages; there is no unique correspondence between well-functioning institutions and the form that such institutions take (Berkowitz et al. 2003; Djankov et al. 2003; Evans 2004; Mukand and Rodrik 2005; Dixit 2007; Rodrik 2007). Therefore, reformers must creatively package those principles into institutional designs that are sensitive to local constraints and take advantage of local opportunities.

---

[2]As explained at length by Scharpf (2010), a substantial asymmetry exists between the clout/scope of the rulings of the European Court of Justice (ECJ)—automatically binding throughout the entire EU—and the high consensus requirements of political action at the European level. It is difficult for member states to protect a national regulation or policy that allegedly impedes any of the four freedoms.

Second, not all institutions that affect entrepreneurial activity can be influenced through policy measures even in the long run. This is true for many informal institutions, such as trust and reputation (Greif 2005) or the way people speak of businessmen and entrepreneurs (McCloskey 2016). Affecting these institutions by means of policy may only be possible through indirect means, as these institutions often only change incrementally over time and/or through bottom-up processes that may be rapid but difficult to anticipate and engineer.

The sharp difference in the initial conditions of member states is a third reason why the first-best approach to institutional reform may become problematic. Countries around the world obviously differ greatly in their capacity to achieve high standards of living for their citizens. In the European Union, GDP per capita in the richest member countries (Ireland and the Netherlands) is two to three times higher than that in the poorest EU countries (Romania and Bulgaria). On a deeper level, each of the Union's 28 member countries has evolved its particular bundle of institutions, many of which are complementary to one another. According to the *varieties of capitalism* (VoC) perspective (Hall and Soskice 2001), institutional complementarities mean that one cannot simply adopt institutions that work well in another country and expect them to work in the same way in a different institutional context. Instead, a prudent and viable reform approach must acknowledge these complexities, or change might become unpredictable or even detrimental to entrepreneurship and economic development. This challenge may explain, for example, why European attempts to imitate policies aimed at stimulating venture capital have (thus far) been unsuccessful (European Commission 2011, 2013). Reforms that fail to take institutional complementarities into account risk rendering the overall institutional system less efficient (Braunerhjelm and Henrekson 2016; Rodrik 2008).

The use of the VoC perspective also allows us to highlight the limitations of our analysis. For example, institutional complementarities are not necessarily confined by the borders of national polities but can work across borders (as in the case of the EU itself) as well as within them. Concerning the latter, institutions at the local level are certainly important. Granted, they commonly evolve and operate against the backdrop of the national institutional framework, particularly in non-federal states, but local initiatives and policies have plenty of room to influence the local entrepreneurial climate in any country.[3] While such considerations are important to recognize, they are beyond the scope of this study, which instead focuses on the national (and supranational) level of political reform.[4]

These problems do not reduce the need for an institutional climate in Europe that is more conducive to entrepreneurship, and they should not make us lose sight of policy liberalization as a long-term goal for the promotion of entrepreneurship and

---

[3]This pertains to both formal institutions, such as taxes (e.g., Haughwout et al. 2004) and regulations (Tannenwald 1997), and to informal institutions, such as the attitudes and social legitimacy derived from entrepreneurship (Elert 2014).

[4]Regarding local institutions that foster entrepreneurship, the reader is referred to Andersson and Henrekson (2015), and Stam and Bosma (2015).

innovation in Europe. Properly acknowledged, these issues can inspire humility and hope regarding what can be achieved in both the short and long terms. They should lead to the recognition that the reform journeys that countries undertake may look very different—more or less bumpy, long and winding, etc.—even though they ought to lead in the same basic direction (if not to the same endpoint). It is beyond the scope of this study to develop a detailed reform roadmap for each EU country, let alone account for regional differences within these countries. Therefore, we seek to identify the general direction that should be taken while emphasizing those differences between the EU countries that must be reckoned with by those assigned to suggest or implement specific reform packages.

The remainder of the study is structured as follows. In Chap. 2, we define and discuss what we mean by the type of entrepreneurship that European countries should strive towards in order to promote innovation. We also identify the actors/functions/competencies in the economy that, in addition to the entrepreneur, are relevant to yielding the desired results. Furthermore, we discuss the VoC approach and how it informs our analysis. In Chap. 3, we draw on these insights and discuss the institutional prerequisites for the development of a vibrant entrepreneurial economy or entrepreneurial ecosystem. Our analysis suggests how institutional framework conditions ought to be improved and how such policy changes will depend on countries' differing starting conditions and institutional complementarities. Finally, in Chap. 4, we provide a summary of the argument and present our main conclusions.

References

Acs, Z. J., Audretsch, D. B., Braunerhjelm, P., & Carlsson, B. (2009). The knowledge spillover theory of entrepreneurship. *Small Business Economics, 32*(1), 15–30.

Acs, Z. J., Desai, S., & Hessels, J. (2008). Entrepreneurship, economic development, and institutions. *Small Business Economics, 31*(3), 219–234.

Aldrich, D. P. (2011). Ties that bond, ties that build: Social capital and governments in post disaster recovery. *Studies in Emergent Order, 4*(December), 58–68.

Andersson, M., & Henrekson, M. (2015). Local competitiveness fostered through local institutions for entrepreneurship. In D. B. Audretsch, A. N. Link, & M. L. Walshok (Eds.), *Oxford handbook of local competitiveness*. Oxford and New York: Oxford University Press.

Åslund, A., & Djankov, S. (2017). *Europe's growth challenge*. Oxford: Oxford University Press.

Baumol, W. J. (1990). Entrepreneurship: Productive, unproductive, and destructive. *Journal of Political Economy, 98*(5), 893–921.

Baumol, W. J. (2010). *The microtheory of innovative entrepreneurship*. Princeton, NJ: Princeton University Press.

Béchard, J.-P., & Grégoire, D. (2005). Entrepreneurship education research revisited: The case of higher education. *Academy of Management Learning and Education, 4*(1), 22–43.

Berkowitz, D., Pistor, K., & Richard, J.-F. (2003). Economic development, legality, and the transplant effect. *European Economic Review, 47*(1), 165–195.

Bhidé, A. (2008). *The venturesome economy: How innovation sustains prosperity in a more connected world*. Princeton, NJ: Princeton University Press.

Bjørnskov, C., & Foss, N. J. (2013). How strategic entrepreneurship and the institutional context drive economic growth. *Strategic Entrepreneurship Journal, 7*(1), 50–69.

Braunerhjelm, P., & Henrekson, M. (2016). An innovation policy framework: Bridging the gap between industrial dynamics and growth. In D. B. Audretsch & A. N. Link (Eds.), *Essays in public sector entrepreneurship*. New York: Springer.

Dixit, A. K. (2007). *Lawlessness and economics: Alternative modes of governance*. Princeton, NJ: Princeton University Press.

Djankov, S., Glaeser, E., La Porta, R., Lopez-de-Silanes, F., & Shleifer, A. (2003). The new comparative economics. *Journal of Comparative Economics, 31*(4), 595–619.

Elert, N. (2014). What determines entry? Evidence from Sweden. *Annals of Regional Science, 53*(1), 55–92.

Estrin, S., Korosteleva, J., & Mickiewicz, T. (2013). Which institutions encourage entrepreneurial growth aspirations? *Journal of Business Venturing, 28*(4), 564–580.

European Commission (2011). *The entrepreneurship 2020 action plan*. Brussels: European Commission.

European Commission (2013). *Entrepreneurship 2020 action plan: Reigniting the entrepreneurial spirit in Europe*. Brussels: European Commission.

European Commission (2015). *Why do we need an Innovation Union?* http://ec.europa.eu/research/innovation-union/index_en.cfm?pg=why. Accessed June 1, 2016.

European Union (2016). *European Innovation Scoreboard 2016*. Brussels: European Commission, Directorate-General for Internal Market, Industry, Entrepreneurship and SMEs.

Evans, P. (2004). Development as institutional change: The Pitfalls of monocropping and the potentials of deliberation. *Studies in Comparative International Development, 38*(4), 30–52.

Friedman, B. M. (2005). *The moral consequences of economic growth*. New York, NY: Alfred A. Knopf.

Greif, A. (2005). Commitment, coercion and markets: The nature and dynamics of institutions supporting exchange. In C. Ménard & M. M. Shirley (Eds.), *Handbook of new institutional economics*. New York: Springer.

Hall, P. A., & Soskice, D. (2001). *Varieties of capitalism: The institutional foundations of comparative advantage*. Oxford: Oxford University Press.

Hall, R. E., & Jones, C. I. (1999). Why do some countries produce so much more output per worker than others? *Quarterly Journal of Economics, 114*(1), 83–116.

Haughwout, A., Inman, R., Craig, S., & Luce, T. (2004). Local revenue hills: Evidence from four U.S. cities. *Review of Economics and Statistics, 86*(2), 570–585.

Henrekson, M., & Johansson, D. (2009). Competencies and institutions fostering high-growth firms. *Foundations and Trends in Entrepreneurship, 5*(1), 1–82.

Hwang, H., & Powell, W. W. (2005). Institutions and entrepreneurship. In S. A. Alvarez, R. Agarwal, & O. Sorenson (Eds.), *Handbook of entrepreneurship research: Disciplinary perspectives*. New York: Springer.

McCloskey, D. N. (2016). *Bourgeois equality: How ideas, not capital or institutions, enriched the world*. Chicago, IL: University of Chicago Press.

Mueller, S. L., & Thomas, A. S. (2000). Culture and entrepreneurial potential: A nine-country study of locus of control and innovativeness. *Journal of Business Venturing, 16*(1), 51–75.

Mukand, S. W., & Rodrik, D. (2005). In search of the holy grail: Policy convergence, experimentation, and economic performance. *American Economic Review, 95*(1), 374–383.

Rodrik, D. (2007). *One economics, many recipes: Globalization, institutions, and economic growth*. Princeton, NJ and Oxford: Princeton University Press.

Rodrik, D. (2008). Second-best institutions. *American Economic Review, 98*(2), 100–104.

Scharpf, F. W. (2010). The asymmetry of European integration, or why the EU cannot be a 'Social Market Economy'. *Socio-Economic Review, 8*(2), 211–250.

Stam, E., & Bosma, N. (2015). Local policies for high-growth firms. In D. B. Audretsch, A. N. Link, & M. L. Walshok (Eds.), *The Oxford handbook of local competitiveness*. Oxford and New York: Oxford University Press.

Tannenwald, R. (1997). State regulatory policy and economic development. *New England Economic Review,* March/April, 83–107.

Urbano, D., & Alvarez, C. (2014). Institutional dimensions and entrepreneurial activity: An international study. *Small Business Economics, 42*(4), 703–716.

Chapter 2
Innovation, Entrepreneurship and the Complementary Skill Structure

Abstract This chapter provides a theoretical foundation to help identify the areas where the need for reform is the greatest. The theories of the experimentally organized economy and of entrepreneurial ecosystems are used to identify six competencies, in addition to that of the entrepreneur, that are necessary for ideas to be generated, identified, selected and commercialized. The competencies are those of inventors, professional managers, competent employees, venture capitalists, actors in secondary markets, and demanding customers. Importantly, no one is in charge of the ecosystem's skill structure, which limits what can be achieved through top-down reform. We also draw on the varieties of capitalism literature, which identifies institutional complementarities as an important driver of the persistent institutional differences across polities. The existence of institutional complementarities implies that viable policy changes must be compatible with existing institutional patterns and that a specific change will have effects that extend throughout the institutional system. As such, they help explain both grid-locks and cascading changes.

Keywords Coordinated market economy · Entrepreneurial ecosystem · Experimentally organized economy · Institutional complementarity · Liberal market economy · Skill structure · Varieties of capitalism

Since Joseph Schumpeter's (1934) seminal work, the view that an economy's long-term growth depends on its ability to exploit innovations has become commonplace (Cohen 2010). Creating these innovations is typically seen as the role of the entrepreneur, whom Schumpeter came to view as the *primus motor* of economic growth. However, entrepreneurs do not operate alone or in a vacuum; they depend on a broader entrepreneurial ecosystem: a skill structure consisting of an array of actors with complementary skills and resources to realize their ideas (Johansson 2009). Furthermore, all actors in the ecosystem's skill structure are constrained and enabled by their institutional environment (Aldrich 2011; Estrin et al. 2013). In this chapter, we present our definition of entrepreneurship and consider how it differs across Europe. We then present the skill structure's other actors, who are necessary to reap the full benefits of innovations and their subsequent commercialization. Lastly, we will discuss the VoC perspective and what it entails for the remainder of our analysis.

© The Author(s) 2017   9
N. Elert et al., *Institutional Reform for Innovation and Entrepreneurship*,
SpringerBriefs in Economics, DOI 10.1007/978-3-319-55092-3_2

2.1 Entrepreneurship in Europe—A First Glance

Today, the importance of entrepreneurship is generally undisputed (Lazear 2005; Baumol 2010; Carree and Thurik 2010), but its definition and measurement remain topics of considerable debate. While an economy's self-employment rate, startup rate or business ownership rate are frequently used as empirical measures of its aggregate entrepreneurial activity, most small and new businesses are best characterized as permanently small. They seldom have any ambition to grow and should not be mistaken for nascent entrepreneurial firms (Hurst and Pugsley 2011; Nightingale and Coad 2014). Researchers increasingly emphasize the need to focus on measures that adequately capture innovative and growth-oriented entrepreneurship (Shane 2009; Stam et al. 2012; Henrekson and Sanandaji 2014). They also focus on the distinction between opportunity and necessity entrepreneurship— that is, whether one becomes an entrepreneur because of a potent business idea or for other reasons, such as a lack of a better means to earn a living (Vivarelli 2013). What matters are the *qualitative* aspects of entrepreneurship, and empirical evidence suggests that an economy that fosters (a few) high-growth firms and high-impact entrepreneurial firms grows faster than an economy that tries to maximize the number of Small and Medium-sized Enterprises (SMEs) or the self-employment rate (Shane 2008; Henrekson and Sanandaji 2014).

We adopt a definition of entrepreneurship that is geared towards making it essential to innovation and economic growth. In line with Henrekson and Stenkula (2016) and closely related to Wennekers and Thurik (1999), we define entrepreneurship as the ability and willingness of individuals, both independently and within organizations,

- to discover and create new economic opportunities;
- to introduce their ideas into the market under uncertainty, making decisions regarding the location, product design, use of resources and reward systems; and
- to create value, which often, though not always, means that the entrepreneur aims to expand the firm to its full potential.[1]

A good first approximation of the prevalence of this type (or possibly these types) of entrepreneurship in Europe is provided by two measures from the annual Global Entrepreneurship Monitor (GEM) surveys. The first measure, *high-growth expectation early-stage entrepreneurship*, is the percentage of an economy's total

---

[1]This is not to deny that there are motives other than monetary gain to become an entrepreneur. Many entrepreneurs have an intrinsic desire to produce a valued good or service and to outcompete other entrepreneurs (Baumol 2002; Manish and Sutter 2016). However, the pursuit of economic gain has a central function even in this case as the accumulation of net assets is a necessary means for an entrepreneur who wants to expand and attain a leading position in the marketplace. It also serves as the yardstick for comparing how successful one's business is relative to others.

entrepreneurial activity (TEA)[2] in which the entrepreneur expects to grow to employ at least five employees within five years. The second measure, *improvement-driven opportunity entrepreneurship*, is the percentage of those involved in TEA (i) who claim to be driven by opportunity as opposed to finding no other option for work, and (ii) who indicate that their chief motives for becoming involved in this opportunity are gaining independence or increasing their income rather than just maintaining it.

Table 2.1 presents the correlation between these measures, the Union's innovation index and PPP-adjusted GDP per capita for the 23 EU member states for which there are data for 2014. High-growth expectation early-stage entrepreneurship is the only measure not to have a strong positive correlation with the others; it is virtually uncorrelated with improvement-driven opportunity entrepreneurship and negatively correlated with innovation and GDP per capita.[3]

Although high-growth expectation early-stage entrepreneurship fails to exhibit a positive correlation with innovation and GDP per capita, it may still be important for countries at a lower level of economic development.[4] Figure 2.1 presents the average *country scores* for the two GEM measures over the period 2010–2014. As a point of comparison, we include numbers for the United States, which is noteworthy for its high scores on both measures. While some EU countries, such as the Czech Republic and Slovenia, also score highly on both measures, the correlation is nonexistent in this sample as well ($r = -0.085$). Some countries, such as Poland, Greece and Spain, score low on both measures, while others have a high score on one measure but a low score on the other. This scatterplot suggests that the way in which entrepreneurship manifests itself differs considerably across European countries.

---

[2]TEA is defined as the proportion of working-age adults (18–64) in the population who either are involved in the process of founding a firm or are active owner-managers of firms that are less than 3.5 years old.

[3]If high-growth expectation early-stage entrepreneurship and improvement-driven opportunity entrepreneurship are instead calculated as a share of the population, the positive correlation between improvement-driven opportunity entrepreneurship and innovation as well as between improvement-driven opportunity entrepreneurship and GDP per capita disappears. There is now also a strong positive correlation between the two entrepreneurship measures. This underscores that analyses of empirical measures of entrepreneurship should be conducted with caution since the specific measure of entrepreneurship used might substantially influence the analysis. However, we deem that focusing on the share of TEA that is growth-oriented and improvement-driven is more relevant in our case since the total TEA in each country differs depending on a number of historical and structural factors.

[4]However, an entrepreneur's assertion that (s)he expects to employ at least five employees does not mean that these plans will be realized. Another relevant measure of entrepreneurship could therefore focus on the prevalence of startups that actually have expanded and hired people. Research has shown that so-called gazelles, i.e., new firms with a high growth rate, are important for economic development (see, e.g., Henrekson and Johansson 2010; Haltiwanger et al. 2013; Coad et al. 2014).

Table 2.1 The correlation between per capita income, innovativeness and the two GEM measures of entrepreneurship

	Innovation index	GDP per capita	High-growth expec. early-stage e-ship	Improvement-driven opportunity e-ship
Innovation index	1.00			
GDP per capita	0.80[b]	1.00		
High-growth expectation early-stage e-ship	−0.40[a]	−0.36[a]	1.00	
Improvement-driven opportunity e-ship	0.51[b]	0.42[a]	−0.09	1.00

Note The innovation index is defined by the European Innovation Scoreboard; GDP per capita is in current PPP dollars for 2015. [b] and [a] denote statistical significance at the 1 and 5% level, respectively
Source Eurostat and Global Entrepreneurship Monitor

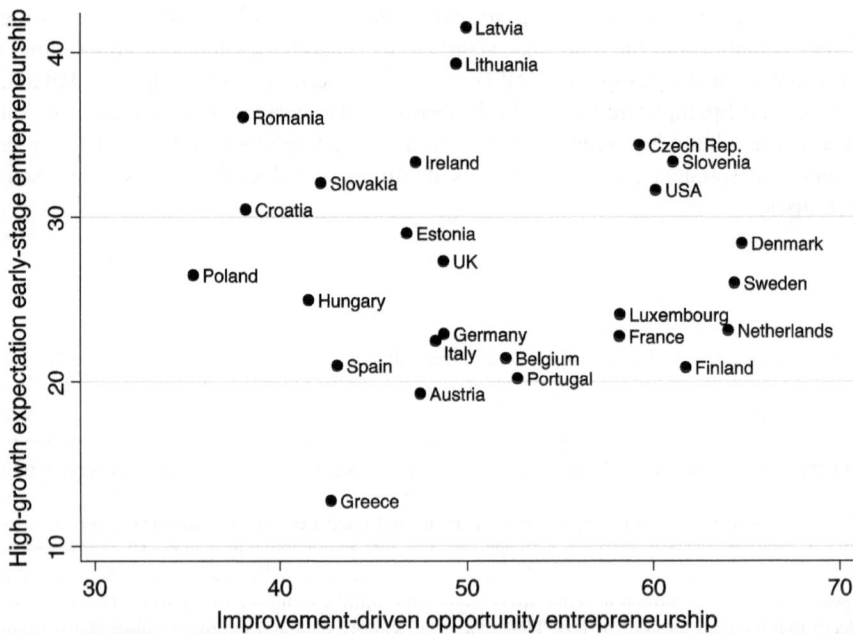

Fig. 2.1 Improvement-driven opportunity and high-growth expectation early-stage entrepreneurship in European countries and the United States, 2010–2014. *Note* Defined as the percentage of all entrepreneurs (TEA) that claim to qualify for either or both types of entrepreneurship. *Source* Global Entrepreneurship Monitor

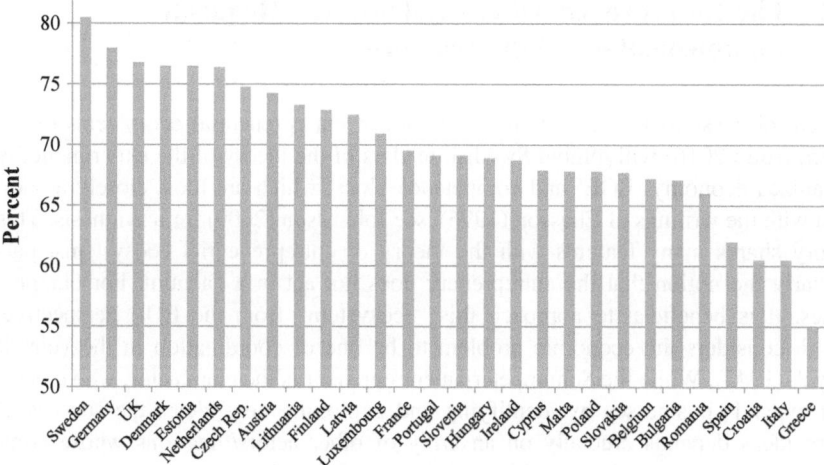

Fig. 2.2 Employment share in 2015 among people aged 20–64 in EU countries. *Note* There are no data for the U.S. for the 20–64-year olds. However, in the OECD data, which reports employment rates for 15–64-year olds, the U.S. employment rate was 68.7% in 2015, compared to 75.5% in top-ranked Sweden and 50.8% in Greece, which has the lowest employment rate among 15–64-year olds. *Source* OECD

As an additional illustration of the differences in starting conditions, Fig. 2.2 shows the large EU cross-country variation in the need for job creation, captured by the employment rate; it varies from 55% in Greece to approximately 80% in Sweden. Furthermore, we see that the rate of high-growth expectation early-stage entrepreneurship is high in several countries with low levels of aggregate employment (Greece is an exception, scoring low on both entrepreneurship measures and employment). Thus, the good news is that there are many entrepreneurs who aim for high growth in these countries; the bad news is that this is insufficient to close the employment gap vis-a-vis other countries with high employment rates.

For countries with low employment rates, notably the three Mediterranean countries, more necessity entrepreneurship is needed to create jobs in the formal sector. Additionally, these member countries can (and do) compensate to some extent for their lower employment rates by having larger shadow (or underground) economies (Schneider 2015; see Appendix Fig. A.2). In Bulgaria and Romania, the shadow economy is estimated to be approximately 30% of official GDP, while the proportion is less than half that in the Northern European countries. However, activity in the shadow economy is generally a poor substitute for activity in the formal sector, partly because it creates unfair competition with firms that do adhere to rules and regulations. More importantly, firms in the shadow economy cannot benefit from the division of labor and specialization to the same extent as formal firms. They are therefore unlikely to grow beyond a small size. Foremost, they should be considered a means of poverty alleviation (La Porta and Shleifer 2008) and a treatment of symptoms rather than a cure for an ailing institutional framework.

2.2 The Entrepreneurial Ecosystem: The Requisite Complementary Skill Structure

Recent discussions in the scientific literature of entrepreneurial ecosystems (Stam 2015; Autio 2016) will remind Swedish readers of the theory of the experimentally organized economy (EOE) and competence blocs, which are most closely associated with the writings of Eliasson (1996); see Johansson (2009) for a synthesis. This theory shares many features with the theory of entrepreneurial ecosystems, particularly the notion that the entrepreneur does not act in a vacuum. For our purposes, it is beneficial to approach this "ecosystem" from the EOE perspective, which considers the economic problem to be one of coordination in the vein of Hayek (1945). While the Schumpeterian entrepreneur is the main actor, who creates and expands businesses by identifying and exploiting new ideas, the success of these ideas depends crucially on an array of other actors/functions whose complementary competencies and inputs are necessary to create and use productive knowledge.

In addition to that of the entrepreneur, the EOE literature identifies at least six competencies that are necessary to generate, identify, select and commercialize ideas. These competencies exist and are deployed (to varying degrees) in virtually all market-based economies. This results in varying outcomes in terms of what type of entrepreneurial ecosystem is produced and ultimately what type of innovative output is realized. In our updated interpretation, the following actors and competencies constitute what we call the *skill structure* in a well-functioning entrepreneurial ecosystem:

   (i) *Inventors*. Entrepreneurs generally have a good overall understanding of how to exploit an opportunity, but they may lack highly specific knowledge regarding the relevant technologies. Inventors may create the foundation for a firm through an invention (patented or not) or work to solve specific problems.

  (ii) *Professional managers*. Professional managers are needed to take commercialization beyond the initial entrepreneurial phase and to organize the expansion of the original venture into a large-scale operation.

 (iii) *Competent employees*. Economic development and growth requires skilled specialists, production staff and front-line personnel. The functioning of the labor market and the educational system is crucial for supplying firms with workers with relevant skills.

 (iv) *Venture capitalists*. They are either business angels or venture capital firms who finance firms and entrepreneurs with "intelligent" capital in the early phases of development. They identify entrepreneurs and their projects, determine whether and how much to invest and decide how the investment should be valued. In this process, they also provide the firm with industry experience, valuable contacts and management skills.

(v) *Actors in secondary markets.* They can be portfolio investors, buy-out firms, management buy-ins or wealthy industrialists who become controlling owners. Their skills and functions are similar to those of venture capitalists, but they operate later in a firm's lifecycle. They assess the value of firms, contribute capital and evaluate the competence of the owner(s) and management. They also help entrepreneurs and venture capitalists reduce or terminate their involvement as the firm moves into a more mature stage.

(vi) *Demanding customers.* Consumption is the ultimate goal of production, and for growth to occur, the products produced must be what consumers demand. The most demanding consumers/clients function as particularly crucial sources of information regarding consumer needs and preferences. One important entrepreneurial skill is thus identifying and cooperating with the right customers.[5]

The ecosystem's skill structure is complete when it has acquired enough critical mass to attract competent actors to a sufficient degree to fulfill each function. A lack of requisite competencies or an important actor category may significantly impede or even prevent the entrepreneurial process from taking place. In a stylized manner, Fig. 2.3 attempts to capture the phases during which the various actors in the skill structure participate in the commercialization process, from the conception and development of an idea through commercialization to full-scale industrialization.

Certainly, the details of the commercialization process vary, and the same person can fulfill more than one role in the skill structure. Oftentimes, the process begins when the entrepreneur identifies a potential opportunity in interactions with demanding customers, which (s)he then strives to develop into an idea that can be commercialized. However, entrepreneurship may also involve creating something that customers have yet to imagine and are thus unable to demand. Additionally, while inventors are commonly involved in resolving technical problems, they can sometimes also initiate a process that is then further developed by the entrepreneur.

Generally, the early commercialization phase mainly involves entrepreneurs and, to a lesser extent, competent employees, while the business angels and venture capital firms finance development.[6] In the scale-up phase, professional managers become involved, together with a greater number of competent employees, while actors in secondary markets assume responsibility for financing, which (depending on sector) might be substantial at this point. Moreover, actors can work alongside each other or overlap during different phases, and professional managers and actors in the secondary market can be involved at an earlier stage, while the entrepreneur may at times also assume the role of inventor or professional manager.

---

[5]In some industries, innovation is largely driven by the users (customers) rather than by firms. This user role is particularly common in industries that produce technical appliances and scientific instruments (see von Hippel et al. 2011).

[6]This does not exclude family, friends and maverick enthusiasts, but the focus here is on professional finance.

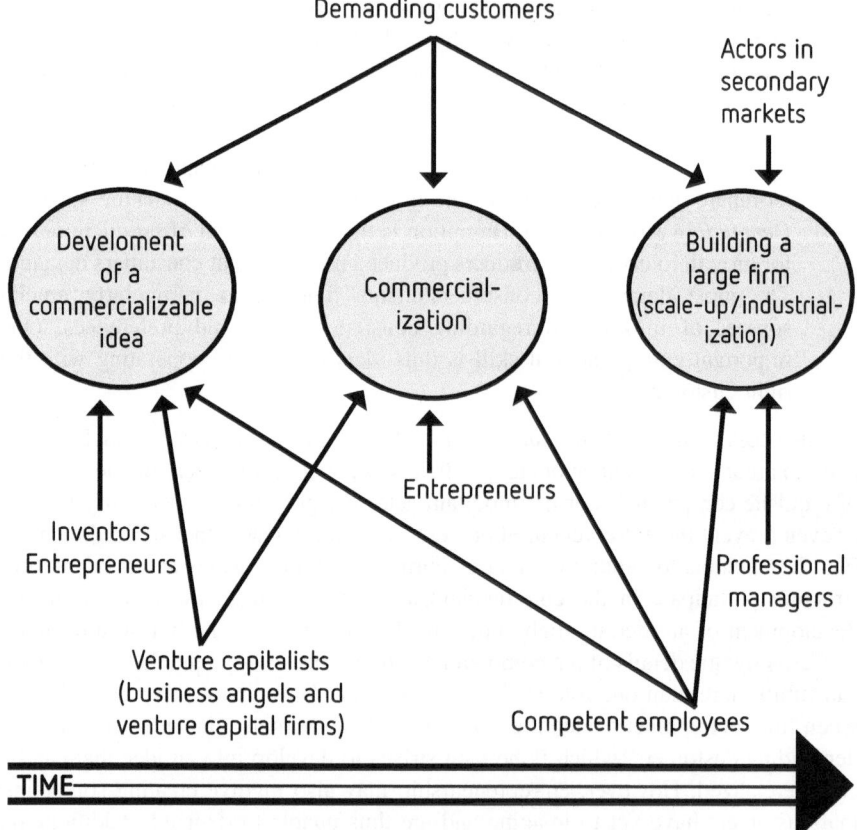

Fig. 2.3 The skill structure: from a concept to a large-scale firm. *Source* Adaptation from Eliasson (1996) and Henrekson and Johansson (2009)

The ecosystem's skill structure is useful when tracing the institutional underpinnings of an entrepreneurial regime because the activities of its actors depend crucially on a society's "rules of the game" (North 1990; Johansson 2009, p. 187). Some institutions are relevant to all actors. Obvious examples are the protection of private property rights, the rule of law and a high level of generalized trust. Other institutions are more competence-specific and mainly affect the broader entrepreneurial system through their effect on that competence. Venture capitalists, for example, obviously depend directly on the institutions underpinning finance and the venture capital industry, whereas the availability of competent employees depends more directly on the functioning of the labor market, the incentives for investing in human capital and the quality of the educational system.

The EOE perspective takes for granted that no specific agent in the ecosystem's skill structure is in charge; no one "owns it" or understands more than a fraction of its inner workings. This is also emphasized in the broader discussion of entrepreneurial ecosystems (Autio 2016) with the implication that no one necessarily feels responsible for ascertaining the efficient functioning of the ecosystem. Thus, traditional "top-down" policy approaches are unlikely to work well (Goldfarb and Henrekson 2003; Acs et al. 2014; Autio and Levie 2016) since they "build on the assumption that it is possible to identify clear-cut 'failures' in the functioning of a given market or an innovation system" and that such failures "can be fixed through top-down intervention" (Autio 2016, p. 22). The very lack of ownership of the entrepreneurial ecosystem means that there is no chain of command that can be applied, which is a central reason that a top-down "command-and-control" approach is unlikely to work or at least should be undertaken with great humility.[7]

In principle, entrepreneurship can be encouraged by efforts ranging from specific targeted support, such as technology assistance to small firms, to general macro policies aimed at maintaining a stable economic environment. Our definition of entrepreneurship in Sect. 2.1 precludes an entrepreneurship policy that is mainly focused on encouraging self-employment or small business activity, often referred to as SME policy. Moreover, as it is difficult—if not impossible—for policymakers to a priori determine who will become an entrepreneur (let alone a successful one), measures directed at a specific group (such as the unemployed) or a specific form of business (such as small or new firms) are largely misdirected (Holtz-Eakin 2000; Lerner 2009). If anything, such measures make for a complex system with detailed rules, exceptions and exceptions to the exceptions. They also result in increased administration and information costs that are almost always more burdensome for small and medium-sized firms (European Commission 2007, 2008). Furthermore, such programs invariably provide opportunities for unproductive and destructive entrepreneurship.

Since few (potential) innovations are Pareto superior, there have been important self-serving interests (such as guilds and unions) throughout history that stood to lose from the introduction of such innovations, usually because those interests owned specific assets dedicated to the state-of-the-art mode of production. An asset used in a highly specialized activity can rarely be reallocated to another activity without incurring substantial costs regardless of whether it consists of physical, human or intangible capital (Caballero 2007). Thus, the value of the asset is contingent on its continued use precisely in its specialized activity. To protect the value of their assets, special interests resort to using non-market means to block the market's selection process, including (notably) legal measures in the form of laws and regulations barring the innovation in question (Olson 1982; Bauer 1995; Mokyr 1998). Regardless of the efficiency of an institution, its beneficiaries thwart change

---

[7]This was already observed by Smith (1966/1759, pp. 342–343) who warned against succumbing to the temptation of thinking like a "man of the system", who thinks he can "arrange the different members of a great society with as much ease as the hand arranges the different pieces upon a chess-board".

to preserve their rents, causing it to become entrenched and non-adaptive over time (Etzioni 1985). To avoid having to fight the same battle time and time again, such interests may have built in an anti-innovation bias into the existing institutional structure.

Therefore, public policy should not try to influence the "natural" evolution of firm size, growth, or form through targeted subsidies or tax breaks. Instead, it should leave this evolution to market forces and profit motives.[8] Policy should aim to support or develop an institutional system that encourages socially productive entrepreneurial activity irrespective of business form and enables the creation and commercialization of valuable knowledge (Acs and Szerb 2007; Braunerhjelm et al. 2010). Whether this implies a high or low rate of self-employment or of SMEs is largely irrelevant.

2.3   Diverse Capitalisms in the European Union

There is considerable institutional diversity even among advanced countries; the United States, Japan and European countries have markedly different models of capitalism, none of which can be declared a clear "winner" (Hall and Soskice 2001; Freeman 2002; Amable 2003). While top-down and bottom-up convergence has occurred in EU countries over the years, member states still differ substantially in their institutional organization, and this diversity is evident even among countries with similar levels of real income. Such differences among countries are not surprising given the documented importance of historical values and norms, lock-in effects and path dependence in institutional evolution (Arthur 1989; Reher 1998; Acemoglu et al. 2001; Nunn 2009; Galasso and Profeta 2011; Giuliano and Nunn 2013; Alesina et al. 2015).

This diversity is a common starting point in the various incarnations of the varieties of capitalism (VoC) literature, which is closely associated with the seminal work of Hall and Soskice (2001). In this literature, institutional complementarities are considered a main driver of the persistence of institutional differences across VoCs. Institutions are complementary if the presence or efficiency of one institution increases the returns from or efficiency of the other. Put simply, if we observe that institution X_A is working well in country A, we cannot assume that copying and then

---

[8]Some authors do admit a role for targeted support. Autio and Rannikko (2016) summarize collected insights, arguing that policy measures that are effective in supporting high-growth firms should be: (1) highly selective, requiring strong, verified growth ambition and some evidence of growth ability as an initial selection criteria; (2) progressive, tying continued support to progressively more demanding milestones that the selected companies should be required to obtain; (3) highly hands-on, emphasizing active, capacity-boosting measures rather than a passive provision of resources and general advice; (4) emphasize partnering with specialized private sector service providers to ensure relevance; (5) substantial enough to ensure meaningful chances of achieving tangible outcomes on growth. This list reveals the practical difficulties of getting targeted support to work efficiently.

substituting it for X_B in country B will yield similar results since the efficiency of any variation of the institution X depends on the workings of other institutions that differ across the two countries (say, Y_A and Y_B, and Z_A and Z_B), which in turn may be more or less amenable to reforms (e.g., depending on whether they are formal or informal).

Therefore, "[n]ations with a particular type of coordination in one sphere of the economy should tend to develop complementary practices in other spheres as well" (Hall and Soskice 2001, p. 18), and institutional practices will not be randomly distributed across nations. Rather, we should be able to observe country clustering in the dimensions that distinguish VoCs from one another. For our purposes, the existence of institutional complementarities implies that viable policy changes must be compatible with existing institutional patterns. Complementarity also implies that a specific change will have effects that extend throughout the institutional system. The fear of this type of snowballing can explain the existence of institutional inertia, as even piecemeal changes are blocked for fear that they may lead to major changes (Amable 2003, p. 7; Aoki 2001).[9]

The exact results from the application of the VoC perspective empirically depend on the number of dimensions considered. For example, Hall and Soskice (2001) emphasize a society's approach to coordination as its key distinguishing feature, and therefore put the spotlight on institutions that facilitate coordination by enabling (i) the exchange of information, (ii) the monitoring of behavior and the (iii) sanctioning of defections from cooperation. This framework yields a core distinction between two types of political economies. In liberal market economies (LMEs), firms coordinate their activities primarily via firm hierarchies and competitive market arrangements. In coordinated market economies (CMEs), coordination relies more heavily on non-market relationships.

Subsequent researchers have taken more dimensions into account and offered more fine-grained contributions. For example, Amable (2003) examines how five spheres in the economy complement one another: wage-setting systems and labor markets, product market competition, finance and corporate governance, the welfare state and social protection, and the educational system. Using a combination of factor and cluster analyses, he thereby identifies five capitalist models: the market-based, the continental European, the social-democratic, the Mediterranean, and the Asian. Another closely related school is that of French regulation theory (Boyer 2005), which identifies four types of capitalism: market-oriented, meso-corporatist, state-driven, and social-democratic.

In a recent contribution, Dilli and Elert (2016) undertake an analysis with a scope similar to that of Amable (2003) but in which the main focus is on understanding the complementarities and features of the institutional structures underlying entrepreneurial regimes. They do a stepwise aggregation of data in an analysis covering 22 countries (19 EU-28 countries together with Norway, Switzerland and

---

[9]Typically, losses are also more salient and weigh more heavily on utility than gains (Kahneman and Tversky 1979), which in and of itself breeds resistance to change.

the United States as points of comparison) and apply a multitude of variables. A principal component analysis reveals three empirically relevant entrepreneurial dimensions across countries: necessity-based nascent entrepreneurship, opportunity entrepreneurship, and aspirational entrepreneurship. When these dimensions are included in a cluster analysis together with a number of theoretically and empirically relevant institutional features, countries cluster into no less than six different groups, each with a distinct bundle of entrepreneurial characteristics and institutional attributes.

The main implication of these approaches is that different reform strategies are appropriate to promote entrepreneurship and economic growth in European countries in different clusters. This will inform our own analysis addressing why and how European countries should undertake reforms to promote entrepreneurship and innovation. Although the general direction in which countries should move will be specified with respect to each area in Chap. 3, those paths can differ considerably depending on the initial economic and institutional conditions. Specifically, our contention is that not taking institutional complementarities into account is likely to breed reform failure. Furthermore, the VoC perspective helps us explain the non-random interconnectedness of various institutions, the persistence of institutional forms that are (seemingly) not conducive to entrepreneurship and growth, and thus the prospects for amending these institutions.

References

Acemoglu, D., Johnson, S., & Robinson, J. A. (2001). The colonial origins of comparative development: An empirical investigation. *American Economic Review, 91*(5), 1369–1401.

Acs, Z., Autio, E., & Szerb, L. (2014). National systems of entrepreneurship: Measurement issues and policy implications. *Research Policy, 43*(3), 476–494.

Acs, Z. J., & Szerb, L. (2007). Entrepreneurship, economic growth and public policy. *Small Business Economics, 28*(2–3), 109–122.

Aldrich, D. P. (2011). Ties that bond, ties that build: Social capital and governments in post disaster recovery. *Studies in Emergent Order, 4*(December), 58–68.

Alesina, A. F., Algan, Y., Cahuc, P., & Giuliano, P. (2015). Family values and the regulation of labor. *Journal of the European Economic Association, 13*(4), 599–630.

Amable, B. (2003). *The diversity of modern capitalism*. Oxford: Oxford University Press.

Aoki, M. (2001). *Towards a comparative institutional analysis*. Cambridge, MA: MIT Press.

Arthur, W. B. (1989). Competing technologies, increasing returns, and lock-in by historical events. *Economic Journal, 99*(394), 116–131.

Autio, E. (2016). *Entrepreneurship support in Europe: Trends and challenges*. Technical Report. London: Imperial College.

Autio, E., & Levie, J. (2016). Management of entrepreneurial ecosystems. I&E Working Paper. London: Imperial College Business School.

Autio, E., & Rannikko, H. (2016). Retaining winners: Can policy boost high-growth entrepreneurship? *Research Policy, 45*(1), 42–55.

Bauer, M. (Ed.) (1995). *Resistance to new technology*. Cambridge: Cambridge University Press.

Baumol, W. J. (2002). *The free-market innovation machine: Analyzing the growth miracle of capitalism.* Princeton, NJ: Princeton University Press.

Baumol, W. J. (2010). *The microtheory of innovative entrepreneurship.* Princeton, NJ: Princeton University Press.

Boyer, R. (2005). How and why capitalisms differ. MPIfG Discussion Paper 05/4. Cologne: Max Planck Institute for the Study of Societies.

Braunerhjelm, P., Acs, Z. J., Audretsch, D. B., & Carlsson, B. (2010). The missing link: Knowledge diffusion and entrepreneurship in endogenous growth. *Small Business Economics, 34*(2), 105–125.

Caballero, R. J. (2007). *Specificity and the macroeconomics of restructuring.* Cambridge, MA: MIT Press.

Carree, M. A., & Thurik, A. R. (2010). The impact of entrepreneurship on economic growth. In Z. J. Acs & D. B. Audretsch (Eds.), *Handbook of entrepreneurship research.* New York, NY: Springer.

Coad, A., Daunfeldt, S.-O., Hölzl, W., Johansson, D., & Nightingale, P. (2014). High-growth firms: Introduction to the special section. *Industrial and Corporate Change, 23*(1), 91–112.

Cohen, W. M. (2010). Fifty years of empirical studies of innovative activity and performance. In B. Hall & N. Rosenberg (Eds.), *Handbook of the economics of innovation* (Vol. 1). Amsterdam: North-Holland.

Dilli, S., & Elert, N. (2016). The diversity of entrepreneurial regimes in Europe. IFN Working Paper No. 1118. Stockholm: Research Institute of Industrial Economics.

Eliasson, G. (1996). *Firm objectives, controls and organization. The use of information and the transfer of knowledge within the firm.* Dodrecht: Kluwer.

Estrin, S., Korosteleva, J., & Mickiewicz, T. (2013). Which institutions encourage entrepreneurial growth aspirations? *Journal of Business Venturing, 28*(4), 564–580.

Etzioni, A. (1985). The political economy of imperfect competition. *Journal of Public Policy, 5*(2), 133–150.

European Commission (2007). *Models to reduce the disproportionate regulatory burden on SMEs.* Enterprise and Industry Directorate-General. Report of the Expert Group. Brussels: European Commission.

European Commission (2008). Think small first. A small business act for Europe. DG Enterprise. Brussels: European Commission.

Freeman, R. B. (2002). Single peaked vs. Diversified capitalism: The relation between institutions and economic outcomes. In J. Drèe (Ed.), *Advances in macroeconomic theory.* London: Palgrave.

Galasso, V., & Profeta, P. (2011). When the state mirrors the family: The design of pension systems. Innocenzo Gasparini Institute for Economic Research (IGER) Working Paper. Milan: IGER.

Giuliano, P., & Nunn, N. (2013). The transmission of democracy: From the village to the nation-state. *American Economic Review, 103*(3), 86–92.

Goldfarb, B., & Henrekson, M. (2003). Bottom-up versus top-down policies towards the commercialization of university intellectual property. *Research Policy, 32*(4), 639–658.

Hall, P. A., & Soskice, D. (2001). *Varieties of capitalism: The institutional foundations of comparative advantage.* Oxford: Oxford University Press.

Haltiwanger, J., Jarmin, R. S., & Miranda, J. (2013). Who creates jobs? Small versus large versus young. *Review of Economics and Statistics, 95*(2), 347–361.

Hayek, F. A. (1945). The use of knowledge in society. *American Economic Review, 35*(4), 519–530.

Henrekson, M., & Johansson, D. (2010). Gazelles as job creators: A survey and interpretation of the evidence. *Small Business Economics, 35*(2), 227–244.

Henrekson, M., & Sanandaji, T. (2014). Small business activity does not measure entrepreneurship. *Proceedings of the National Academy of Sciences (PNAS), 111*(5), 1760–1765.

Henrekson, M., & Stenkula, M. (2016). *Understanding entrepreneurship: Definition, function and policy*. Lund: Studentlitteratur.

Holtz-Eakin, D. (2000). Public policy toward entrepreneurship. *Small Business Economics, 15*(4), 283–291.

Hurst, E., & Pugsley, B. W. (2011). What do small businesses do? *Brookings Papers on Economic Activity*, Fall, 73–118.

Johansson, D. (2009). The theory of the experimentally organized economy and competence blocs: An introduction. *Journal of Evolutionary Economics, 20*(2), 185–201.

Kahneman, D., & Tversky, A. (1979). Prospect theory: An analysis of decision under risk. *Econometrica, 47*(2), 263–291.

La Porta, R., & Shleifer, A. (2008). The unofficial economy and economic development. NBER Working Paper No. 14520. Cambridge, MA: National Bureau of Economic Research.

Lazear, E. P. (2005). Entrepreneurship. *Journal of Labor Economics, 23*(4), 649–680.

Lerner, J. (2009). *Boulevard of broken dreams: Why public efforts to boost entrepreneurship and venture capital have failed—And what to do about it*. Princeton, NJ: Princeton University Press.

Manish, G. P., & Sutter, D. (2016). Mastery versus profit as motivation for the entrepreneur: How crony policies shape business. *Journal of Entrepreneurship and Public Policy, 5*(1), 95–112.

Mokyr, J. (1998). The political economy of technological change: Resistance and innovation in economic history. In M. Berg & K. Bruland (Eds.), *Technological revolutions in Europe* (pp. 39–64). Cheltenham, UK and Northampton, MA: Edward Elgar Publishers.

Nightingale, P., & Coad, A. (2014). Muppets and gazelles: Political and methodological biases in entrepreneurship research. *Industrial and Corporate Change, 23*(1), 113–143.

North, D. C. (1990). *Institutions, institutional change and economic performance*. Cambridge: Cambridge University Press.

Nunn, N. (2009). The importance of history for economic development. *Annual Review of Economics, 1*(1), 65–92.

Olson, M. (1982). *The rise and decline of nations: Economic growth, stagflation, and social rigidities*. New Haven, CT: Yale University Press.

Reher, D. S. (1998). Family ties in Western Europe: Persistent contrasts. *Population and Development Review, 24*(2), 203–234.

Schneider, F. (2015). Size and development of the shadow economy of 31 European and 5 other OECD Countries from 2003 to 2015: Different developments. Mimeo. Linz, AUT: Department of Economics, Johannes Kepler University.

Schumpeter, J. A. (1934). *The theory of economic development: An inquiry into profits, capital, credit, interest and the business cycle*. Cambridge, MA: Harvard University Press.

Shane, S. A. (2008). *The illusions of entrepreneurship*. New Haven and London: Yale University Press.

Shane, S. A. (2009). *Fool's gold: The truth behind angel investing in America*. New York: Oxford University Press.

Smith, A. (1966/1759). *Theory of moral sentiments*. New York: Kelley.

Stam, E. (2015). Entrepreneurial ecosystems and regional policy—A sympathetic critique. *European Planning Studies, 23*(9), 1759–1769.

Stam, E., Bosma, N., van Witteloostuijn, A., de Jong, J., Bogaert, S., Edwards, N., et al. (2012). *Ambitious entrepreneurship. A review of the state of the art*. Bryssel: Vlaamse Raad voor Wetenschap en Innovatie.

Vivarelli, M. (2013). Is entrepreneurship necessarily good? Microeconomic evidence from developed and developing countries. *Industrial and Corporate Change, 22*(6), 1453–1495.

von Hippel, E., Ogawa, S., & de Jong, J. P. J. (2011). The age of the consumer-innovator. *MIT Sloan Management Review, 53*(1), 27–35.

Wennekers, S., & Thurik, A. R. (1999). Linking entrepreneurship and economic growth. *Small Business Economics, 13*(1), 27–56.

Chapter 3
Innovation and Entrepreneurship in the European Union—A Reform Agenda

Abstract In this chapter, we discuss the institutions that the previous literature identifies as the most relevant for nurturing the activities of entrepreneurs and other actors in the ecosystem's skill structure. Overall, we discuss nine areas: (i) the rule of law and the protection of property rights; (ii) the tax system; (iii) regulations governing savings, capital and finance; (iv) the organization of labor markets and social insurance systems; (v) regulations governing goods and service markets; (vi) regulations governing bankruptcy and insolvency; (vii) R&D, commercialization and knowledge spillovers; (viii) human capital investments; and (ix) informal institutions. Although our starting point is that some institutions or institutional forms are simply the most propitious for entrepreneurship and economic growth, we complement this first-best perspective with insights offered by the perspectives discussed in Chap. 2, and clarify the extent to which policies and institutions interact with and reinforce one another.

Keywords Bankruptcy law · Employment protection legislation · Financing of entrepreneurship · Human capital · Informal institutions · Knowledge spillovers · Product market regulations · Rule of law · Social insurance · Taxation

In this chapter, we discuss the institutions that the previous literature identifies as the most relevant for nurturing the activities of entrepreneurs and other actors in the ecosystem's skill structure. The starting point for this discussion can be labeled the first-best perspective, according to which some institutions or institutional forms are simply the most propitious for entrepreneurship and economic growth. This perspective has rightfully been criticized as too simplistic (Rodrik 2008). McCloskey (2016) quips that it essentially amounts to the idea that one should "add institutions and stir". Hence, we recognize the need to complement it with insights offered by the EOE and the VoC perspectives discussed in the previous chapter.

Previous research suggests that (innovation-based and high-impact) entrepreneurship has numerous important prerequisites, such as an educated workforce (Béchard and Grégoire 2005; Kuratko 2005), a well-functioning labor market (Poschke 2013), and a tax system that favors work, investment and

© The Author(s) 2017
N. Elert et al., *Institutional Reform for Innovation and Entrepreneurship*,
SpringerBriefs in Economics, DOI 10.1007/978-3-319-55092-3_3

entrepreneurial effort (Cullen and Gordon 2007). Giving a complete overview of the large empirical literature that identifies the effect of various institutions and policies on the rate of entrepreneurial activity is beyond the scope of this chapter. However, it is important to make several points clarifying the extent to which policies and institutions (both formal and informal) interact with and reinforce one another. In what follows, we will highlight what we consider to be the most pertinent institutions and policies that determine the extent to which a productive entrepreneurial economy is fostered.

3.1   The Rule of Law and Protection of Property Rights

3.1.1   Preamble

The legal principle that a polity should not be governed by arbitrary decisions made by autocratic rulers or government officials is central to any country striving for prosperity. Likewise, private property rights—the existence of legal titles to hold property and the protection thereof—is arguably the most fundamental of all economic institutions (North and Weingast 1989; Libecap 1993; Acemoglu et al. 2001; Baumol 2002; Rodrik et al. 2004; Acemoglu and Johnson 2005; Besley and Ghatak 2010) and relevant for all actors in the ecosystem's skill structure. Secure property rights ensure that physical objects can be turned into capital (De Soto 2000), a transformation that requires judgment, imagination, and innovation. Without control over assets and their returns, a potential entrepreneur will lack the incentive to innovate, but what matters is de facto control; formal property rights which do not offer control rights in practice are useless, while the absence of formal property rights need not be prohibitive if control rights are sufficiently strong (Rodrik 2007). However, entrepreneurs in countries with weak property rights are generally discouraged from (re)investing (retained) earnings in their ventures; see Johnson et al. (2002). The division and specialization of labor are also hampered, which narrows the range of potential entrepreneurial discoveries.

If the protection of property rights is too weak, destructive entrepreneurship, such as extortion and corruption, is likely to flourish. Organized crime syndicates such as the mafia are often innovative in their response to shortcomings in the legal enforcement framework and pursue entrepreneurship as a substitute for absent or maladaptive public institutions.[1] There are also instances in which innovativeness and entrepreneurship may suffer from overly strong property rights protections (Gans and Persson 2013). An important contemporary example is intellectual

---

[1]The Sicilian Mafia and criminal organizations in Japan illustrate that these activities are not necessarily negative for the economy, given the context within which they are conducted (Milhaupt and West 2000; Bandiera 2003; Douhan and Henrekson 2010). Nevertheless, the weaker the property rights, the more predatory the entrepreneurial activities are likely to be.

property rights protection, which has been strengthened in recent years in ways that are arguably too protective, most notably in the United States, increasing both the cost and risk associated with innovative activity (Jaffe and Lerner 2004; Cohen 2005; Acs and Sanders 2012).

In practice, one must strike a difficult compromise within the legal system. On the one hand, if protection is too weak or can be circumvented too easily (through unproductive or destructive entrepreneurship), there is no incentive to introduce innovations in the first place (Merrill et al. 2004; Acs and Szerb 2007; Baumol et al. 2007; Kauffman Foundation 2007). On the other hand, if protection is overly strong —if its time frame is too long or if it is too easy to obtain even for inventions that are not truly novel—the original innovator will be able to extract excessive monopoly rents, making the economy less competitive and less innovative.

3.1.2 Reform Agenda

Although no country in the world can pride itself on having perfected the rule of law, cross-country differences are substantial. As presented in column 1 of Table 3.1, this is also true among EU countries. The former Soviet-bloc countries score especially low on the rule of law, but this is also true for Greece and Italy and, to a slightly lesser extent, for Spain and Portugal. The top countries are the Nordic, Anglo-Saxon and Benelux nations. These are also the wealthiest EU countries. The second column of the table reveals large differences in terms of the security of property rights as well, and the order of countries is quite similar to the order for the rule of law.

For citizens and economic agents to reap the full benefits of the rule of law, the laws and regulations in question must be of high quality, and the government must be sufficiently effective in maintaining the rule of law. The third and fourth indicators in Table 3.1 show that the differences across EU countries are large in these respects as well. However, it is noteworthy that the quality of the laws and regulations in the laggard countries tend to be higher than the government's effectiveness at enforcing compliance. Arguably, this is not surprising. Adopting the right laws is easier than enforcing them effectively. Furthermore, EU law compels countries to do the former but has far less clout to enforce or ensure the latter.

Regarding the rule of law, the efficiency of government, and the protection of property rights we see no alternative for the laggard countries but to do their utmost to converge towards the level of the best-performing countries. Deficiencies in these factors negatively impact all agents in the ecosystem's skill structure and induce people to conduct activities and keep their capital in the shadow economy. Even the poorest EU member countries are higher medium-income countries, and neither the VoC literature nor arguments à la Rodrik (2008) provide any support for the view that these countries can compensate for these deficiencies through other institutional measures.

Table 3.1 The rule of law and the quality of government: four indicators for the EU member countries and the United States

Country	Rule of law	Security of property rights	Government effectiveness	Regulatory quality
Finland	100.0	8.98	95.1	91.9
Denmark	99.3	7.83	89.2	87.3
Sweden	96.8	7.82	88.8	89.4
Netherlands	96.5	8.07	89.9	88.8
Austria	95.9	8.07	82.6	81.7
Luxembourg	94.4	8.52	85.0	85.6
UK	94.2	8.70	84.0	90.1
Germany	93.3	7.73	87.2	86.7
Ireland	92.0	8.12	83.5	88.2
USA	87.4	7.25	79.5	76.3
Belgium	84.8	7.41	77.9	73.8
France	83.7	7.57	78.0	71.6
Estonia	81.2	6.97	68.1	86.2
Malta	77.2	6.74	67.6	72.1
Czech Rep.	75.5	5.01	67.5	70.1
Portugal	75.3	6.41	67.1	63.8
Cyprus	73.5	5.55	70.6	71.9
Slovenia	71.5	5.30	67.1	61.2
Spain	70.5	5.54	71.1	64.0
Lithuania	69.7	5.41	66.7	74.5
Latvia	68.7	5.99	66.1	73.7
Poland	67.5	5.54	62.0	71.0
Hungary	59.5	4.56	53.9	63.7
Slovakia	58.9	4.74	63.3	67.0
Greece	55.7	4.84	50.0	53.3
Italy	55.5	5.02	49.5	61.1
Croatia	54.9	4.65	58.3	54.7
Romania	50.9	4.93	39.0	59.5
Bulgaria	45.2	4.11	41.6	59.0

Note Rule of law captures perceptions of the extent to which agents have confidence in and abide by the rules of society, in particular the quality of contract enforcement, property rights, the police, and the courts, as well as the likelihood of crime and violence. *Security of property rights* captures the extent to which individuals have secure rights to property, including the fruits of their labor. *Government effectiveness* captures perceptions of the quality of public and civil services and the degree of their independence from political pressures, the quality of policy formulation and implementation, and the credibility of the government's commitment to such policies. *Regulatory quality* captures perceptions of the ability of the government to formulate and implement sound policies and regulations that permit and promote private-sector development. All scores are standardized from 0 to 100, where the value 100 is assigned to the leading country. Singapore is the leading country for the 3rd and 4th measure
Source World Bank, *World Governance Indicators 2015,* and Gwartney et al. (2015) for security of property rights

3.2 Taxation

3.2.1 Preamble

The design of the tax system affects the net return to entrepreneurship both directly and indirectly; it also affects the prevalence and activities of the other actors in the ecosystem's skill structure. The tax system determines a potential entrepreneur's risk-reward profile and, consequently, his or her incentives for undertaking entrepreneurial activities. The literature has consistently found that the self-employed are more responsive to taxes than employees (e.g., Carroll et al. 2000; Rosen 2005; Heim 2010; Chetty et al. 2011; Harju and Kosonen 2013; Alstadsæter et al. 2014; Kleven and Schultz 2014). The elasticity of taxable income is far higher for the self-employed than for employees, which implies that higher taxes reduce the supply of taxable income due to a combination of real effects and tax reporting. However, the effects are often complex and sometimes counterintuitive. From a theoretical point of view, we will focus on two main ways in which the tax system affects entrepreneurial activity.[2]

The first is an *absolute effect* that influences the supply and effort of potential entrepreneurs in the economy, as an absolute increase in the taxation of entrepreneurs lowers the (expected) after-tax reward. It also makes expansion financed by retained earnings more difficult and negatively affects the liquidity position of entrepreneurs. In sum, the absolute effect serves to frustrate entrepreneurial activities and impedes the emergence of new startups and the expansion of firms. The second is a *relative effect* that influences an individual's choice of occupation and organizational form by altering the relative returns for different activities if the tax favors one form of economic activity over another; thus, a higher tax rate may encourage income shifting and may positively influence (some forms of) entrepreneurship in the economy. A relative effect also occurs if the tax system favors certain forms of savings and investments. To the extent that the optimal financing and ownership structures differ across industries, firm type and firm age, such non-neutralities affect incentives for entrepreneurship.[3]

---

[2]See Henrekson and Sanandaji (2016b).

[3]Two additional effects are of less importance for the discussion at hand: an *evasion* effect influencing the willingness to become an entrepreneur to exploit opportunities to decrease the tax burden, which arises if evading taxes on entrepreneurial income, either illegally or legally, is easier than it would be for wage income. Self-employed entrepreneurs may be able to underreport income by neglecting to register cash sales, overstating costs by recording private expenses as business costs, or using informal agreements that are difficult for the tax authority to verify. Higher taxes may therefore encourage self-employment, but tax avoidance opportunities become more difficult to exploit as a business expands. Lastly, there is an *insurance* effect in the case of both proportional and progressive taxation having a full loss offset, as such a scheme functions as insurance that stimulates risk taking (Domar and Musgrave 1944). With respect to entrepreneurship, increased taxation of the net return with a full loss offset will reduce the after-tax variance of profits and therefore the risk associated with the business. If potential entrepreneurs are risk averse, this risk reduction may stimulate entrepreneurship. By contrast, a progressive tax system with an imperfect

While analyzing taxes on entrepreneurial income directly would be preferable, such an analysis is complicated by the fact that no specific tax on income from entrepreneurial effort exists in practice. Rather, this income is taxed in several different forms, notably as labor income, business income, current capital income (dividends and interest), or capital gains. These taxes may affect entrepreneurial activities differently. A thorough analysis of the effects of taxation on entrepreneurship must disentangle these effects, and we do so by enumerating and discussing what we deem to be the key characteristics of a tax system favoring innovative entrepreneurship and the ecosystem's skill structure.

Regarding corporate taxation, a high tax rate on business profits discourages equity financing and encourages debt financing if interest costs are tax-deductible (Desai et al. 2003; Huizinga et al. 2008). To the extent that debt financing is less costly and more readily available to larger firms, high corporate tax rates coupled with tax-deductible interest payments disadvantage smaller firms and potential entrepreneurs (Davis and Henrekson 1999). Taxing corporate profits also reduces the retained earnings that can be used to expand the existing venture. Consequently, taxing profits in small firms often leads to lower growth rates (Michaelas et al. 1999).

A high tax rate on dividends encourages a reliance on retained earnings to finance expansion. Such a tax rate punishes new ventures, locks in retained earnings, and traps capital in incumbent firms. Therefore, a high tax rate on dividends obstructs the flow of capital to the most promising projects because it favors incumbent ventures (Chetty and Saez 2005). Most of the economic return from successful high-impact entrepreneurial firms accrues to owners in the form of a dramatically increased value of their shares rather than as dividends or large interest payments to the owners. Thus, the taxation of capital gains on stock holdings greatly affects the incentives of potential high-impact entrepreneurs and their (equity) financiers (Cumming 2005; Da Rin et al. 2006).

Employee stock options are the equivalent of promises of future ownership stakes in the firm, which will be realized if the firm develops according to plan and manages to achieve the prescribed objectives for value creation. The granting of stock options can also be substituted for high wages to moderate costs at the beginning of the lifecycle (Gompers and Lerner 2001; Bengtsson and Hand 2013). Stock options can thus be used to encourage and reward individuals who supply key competencies to a firm—the competent employees in the ecosystem's skill structure. In ideal circumstances, stock options provide incentives that closely mimic direct ownership, but their productivity greatly depends on the tax code. If gains on stock options are taxed as wage income, some of the incentive effect is lost —particularly if the gains are subject to (uncapped) social security contributions

---

(Footnote 3 continued)

loss offset will deter entrepreneurial business entry since entrepreneurial income is more variable than salaried income, which means that the average tax will be higher for entrepreneurs in a progressive tax system (Gentry and Hubbard 2000).

and the marginal tax rate on wage income is high. The situation changes dramat-ically if an employee with stock options can defer the tax liability until the stocks are eventually sold. The effectiveness of these stock options is further reinforced if the employee suffers no tax consequences from the granting or exercise of the option, and if the employee is taxed at a low capital gains rate when the acquired stock is sold (Gilson and Schizer 2003).

The level and progressivity of labor taxation (including mandatory social security contributions) also affect employees directly by determining the incentives for work effort, labor supply (on the extensive and intensive margin), occupational choice, career aspirations, and the propensity to upgrade and learn new skills (Rosen 1983). Most obviously, high and progressive labor taxes lower the rate of return on highly productive skills, and are therefore likely to impair the supply of skilled workers.[4] They also slow restructuring and the reallocation of people across firms since it becomes costlier to achieve the net wage differential necessary to induce a person to leave their current employment. Hence, high taxation of labor income affects several of the categories in the skill structure, especially competent employees and entrepreneurs. Of course, the supply of competent employees is also affected by the tax incentives to acquire an adequate education, a question to which we will return in Sect. 3.8.[5]

Regarding the role of venture capitalists in the ecosystem's skill structure, we should note that the tax systems of many countries evolved before the emergence of complicated ownership structures involving private equity financing, such as ven-ture capital (VC) and buyout firms.[6] Sophisticated mechanisms were initially needed to provide high-powered incentives for many actors in addition to the final equity holders. In fact, the modern VC industry in the U.S. could not evolve until the tax system was changed in key respects. Sharp reductions in the capital gains tax and legislation pertaining to stock options around 1980 allowed the tax liability to be deferred until stocks were sold rather than when the options were exercised. Additionally, new legislation in 1979 allowed pension funds to invest in high-risk securities that were issued by small or new companies and VC funds (Misher 1984; Fenn et al. 1995).

We should emphasize here that important complementarities exist between different tax rates. For example, the low effective taxation of gains on employee stock options appears to be necessary to develop a large VC sector. In addition, when channeling institutional capital into the entrepreneurial startup sector, finding efficient substitutes for VC firms is difficult. Overall, to calculate the total effect of

---

[4]Although it is difficult to find direct evidence of such an effect, there is highly plausible indirect evidence in the form of high estimates of the elasticity of taxable income at high income levels (Gruber and Saez 2002; Saez et al. 2012).

[5]This issue is discussed at some length in Henrekson and Rosenberg (2001).

[6]Private equity (PE) ownership involves the following layers of ownership: private ownership stakes by founders and key personnel in the portfolio companies, an ownership share by the PE firm and the PE partners (often indirect), several investors' stakes in the PE fund, and final beneficiaries (often current or future retirees) of institutions investing in PE funds.

taxation, one must consider the specific rules for depreciation and valuation in corporate taxation and the taxation of interest income, dividends, capital gains, and wealth. The effective total tax rate also depends on the ownership category. In many developed countries, business ownership stakes that are directly held by individuals and families have been taxed more heavily than other ownership stakes. The wave of tax reforms that swept the OECD in the 1980s reduced many of these differences, but those that remain provoke an endogenous response in the ownership structure of the business sector to the tax-favored owner categories (Rydqvist et al. 2014). If individual stock holdings are disfavored relative to institutional holdings and if institutional investors are less willing to invest in small and new entrepreneurial projects, entrepreneurial activity will be discouraged.

3.2.2   Reform Agenda

In line with the general argument articulated in Sect. 2.2, our contention is that the tax system should strive for as much simplicity as possible rather than addressing shortcomings by granting exceptions and tax breaks for specific ownership types or industries. Tax breaks are often instituted for good reasons, and they may very well appear justified when analyzed in isolation. However, they create complexities with numerous drawbacks. First, they are vulnerable to tax-driven business models that are legal but not in line with the spirit of the concession in question. Moreover, highly complex systems lack in salience. For example, if economic actors can realize a lower effective taxation than the statutory one, it becomes more difficult to achieve the behavioral effects that policymakers would like to see (Chetty et al. 2009).

3.2.2.1   Taxation of Labor Income

As shown in the first column of Table 3.2, the highest marginal tax rates differ greatly across the European Union—spanning from 16% in Hungary to 57% in Sweden. However, the highest marginal tax rate is not necessarily the most relevant measure. One should also examine the total marginal tax wedge, which is defined as the share of total labor cost at the margin and consists of the sum of mandatory social security contributions paid by the employer and/or the employee and the marginal income tax rate. This is performed for different relevant family constellations in columns 2–4 of Table 3.2. In a country like Belgium, as much as two-thirds of total labor cost consists of income taxes and social security contributions, while the share in Poland is only about half as large.

Institutional complementarity can enable a country to tax labor income more heavily without suffering from increased distortionary effects. Most importantly, high labor taxation has less detrimental effects if access to valuable subsidies in cash or in-kind (e.g., child care and pension rights) is tied to employment and if

Table 3.2 Top marginal tax rate on labor income, and marginal rate of income tax plus employee and employer contributions less cash benefits (tax wedge), 2015

Country	Top marginal tax rate on labor income	Single no child, 100% AW	Single, no child, 167% AW	Married, 2 children, 100 and 67% AW
Austria	50.0	60.5	42.2	60.5
Belgium	45.3	66.3	68.5	65.5
Czech Rep.	20.1	48.6	48.6	48.6
Denmark	55.8	42.0	55.8	42.0
Estonia	19.7	41.2	41.2	41.2
Finland	49.1	55.5	58.5	56.2
France	54.0	59.3	59.8	56.4
Germany	47.5	60.2	44.3	57.7
Greece	50.0	47.6	54.8	47.6
Hungary	16.0	49.0	49.0	49.0
Ireland	47.0	55.8	55.8	37.7
Italy	48.8	56.0	63.3	56.6
Luxembourg	43.6	55.5	55.5	53.0
Netherlands	49.2	46.7	52.1	46.7
Poland	20.9	37.2	37.2	37.2
Portugal	50.3	53.9	60.8	51.1
Slovakia	21.7	46.5	46.5	46.5
Slovenia	39.0	51.0	60.4	43.6
Spain	46.0	49.9	38.0	49.9
Sweden	57.0	48.3	67.3	48.3
UK	45.0	40.2	49.0	40.2
USA	46.3	43.6	43.6	34.3

Note AW Average wage. The marginal tax wedge refers to the principal earner with an income of 100% of AW and the secondary earner with an income of 67% of AW in the rightmost column
Source OECD, *Taxing Wages 2014–2015*

each spouse's income is taxed separately rather than jointly (Lindbeck 1982). The importance of the latter effect becomes obvious when comparing the third and fourth columns in Table 3.2 for Belgium and Sweden.

In fact, as mentioned (and as shown in Fig. 2.2 in Sect. 2.1), Sweden has the highest employment rate in the entire EU, but this does not mean that its excessive taxation of high incomes is costless. In fact, a reform to remove taxations of the highest income levels in Sweden would probably more than finance itself (Sørensen 2010). As it stands, these taxes can be expected to have deleterious effects, particularly in the most advanced parts of the economy. In all likelihood, Sweden is successful in employment terms despite rather than because of its high labor taxes, which can only be borne because of the overall quality of the institutional environment. Countries with poorer institutional quality should therefore not see Sweden as a role model in this respect. Poor countries that would like to increase their tax revenue must begin by improving the quality of their basic institutions.

Labor income is taxed at low rates in most Eastern European countries. Nonetheless, these countries have large underground economies, while the employment rate is low, as is the rate of improvement-driven opportunity entrepreneurship. This strongly suggests that factors other than high taxes on labor are binding constraints for this cluster of countries. The situation is different for several of the Mediterranean countries; they also suffer from low employment and entrepreneurship, whereas the underground economy tends to be large. In these countries, as well as in Belgium and France, labor taxation is a clear impediment. Reform is therefore needed to combine lower labor taxes with a stricter coupling of subsidies, such as child care and pension rights, to employment. The latter issues will be addressed in Sect. 3.4.

3.2.2.2   Taxation of Corporate Income

As shown in Fig. 3.1, there are large differences across EU countries in the statutory corporate tax rate, ranging from 34% in France to 12.5% in Ireland. In the case of corporate taxation, we see no reason for the European Union to strive for convergence across EU countries. In this case, healthy institutional competition among member countries is preferred.

This does not preclude an important role for the European Union. First, the Union must be adamant about ending blatant institutional arbitrage and sweetheart deals negotiated between national governments and large multinational corporations. Additionally, the Union should strive to reduce and ideally remove the discrepancies in member countries between statutory and effective corporate income tax rates, which may result from tax-reducing depreciation rules, inventory valuation rules or other more ad hoc country- or industry-specific tax reductions. Their

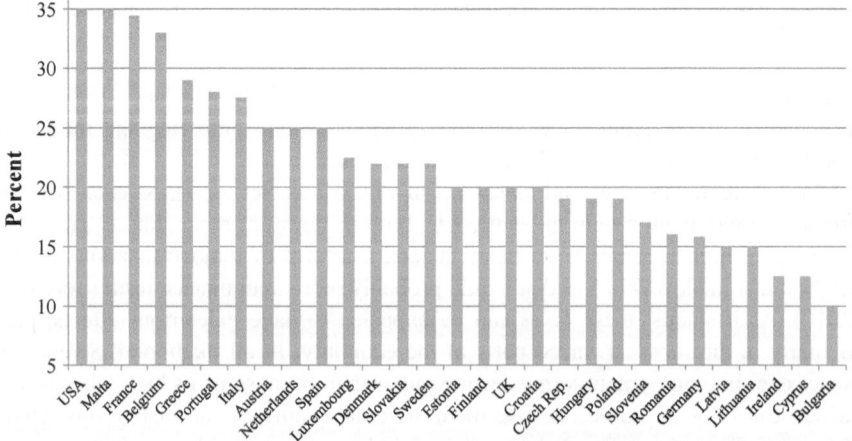

Fig. 3.1 The statutory corporate tax rate in EU countries and the U.S., 2016. *Source* OECD and Eurostat.

removal would create transparency and contribute to leveling the playing field for all firms regardless of their size, industry or nationality. Competition among member states is good, but it should be competition on corporate tax rates and not on complex, opaque fiscal deals and schemes. Member states should treat all firms equally.

3.2.2.3 Taxation of Dividends and Capital Gains

The return on entrepreneurship largely accrues in the form of dividends and capital gains from ownership stakes in the firm. The standard tax rates on dividends and capital gains among EU countries and the United States are given in Appendix Table A.1 and reveal major differences. More importantly, there are country-specific, highly idiosyncratic divergences from these standard rates. These divergences depend on factors such as the holding period, the size of the firm, whether the firm is private or public (i.e., traded on a stock exchange), whether a person is an active or passive owner, whether the firm and/or the investor qualifies for inclusion in a tax-favored scheme (e.g., a scheme geared towards encouraging innovative startup activity), and the tax status of the body (a physical or a juridical person, etc.) receiving the capital income.

As exemplified by Grant (2016), such differences can be huge and vary substantially across countries. In Sweden, the dividend and capital gains tax rates can vary between 20 and 60% for physical persons depending on circumstances, whereas the Irish dividend tax rate varies between 20 and 40% and the Irish capital gains tax rate can be reduced from 33% to zero under certain conditions.[7] On the other hand, the variation is small in the Netherlands, Poland, and Estonia; in the latter country, dividends are taxed at 0% and capital gains at 20%.

The complexities should be removed when possible. Instead, countries should aim for dividend and capital gains tax rates with few exceptions and few (opaque) concessionary schemes. Here, the Eastern European countries, such as Poland and Estonia, have exemplary models in which the tax rates are at reasonable levels and the effective tax rate is largely independent of other circumstances. Arguably, the reason for this clarity is that the design of these systems date back no further than 1989. A radical redesign from the ground up is probably not feasible in older member states, but they should nevertheless strive for similar improvements to simplicity and transparency.

3.2.2.4 Taxation of Stock Options

Observations from the history of the American VC sector indicates that stock options are widely used when they are advantageous from a tax perspective. The

---

[7]See OECD (2015a) for details regarding the taxation of income from SMEs.

contractual design of financial instruments constitutes a good fit for the issues facing the VC-funded entrepreneurial sector. Therefore, the effective tax treatment of option contracts may in itself be a major determinant to the size of the VC-funded entrepreneurial sector. Henrekson and Sanandaji (2016a) calculate the effective tax rate on stock options in various countries given a typical scenario. The tax rates for the EU countries included in their study as well as those for the United States and Hong Kong are presented in Table 3.3, revealing a large variation in tax rates. The VC sector is extremely small in most countries where the tax rate is very high, as will become clear in the next section (see Table 3.4, in particular), while the low-tax countries (Hong Kong and the United States) have a large and highly dynamic VC sector.

Lowered taxation of gains on employee stock options in the startup sector is likely to be necessary in many countries, both to lure talented people away from traditional careers in incumbent firms and to channel institutional capital into the entrepreneurial sector, which should be mediated by a professional VC sector. This policy would narrowly target the entrepreneurial sector rather than entail broad tax cuts (Gilson and Schizer 2003) if designed to apply only to startups receiving VC-funding, a small but strategic sector of the economy. The policy lowers the effective taxation of startups that are screened by venture capitalists willing to invest their own funds without requiring the government to determine which firms are entrepreneurial. Innovative startups can then be favored without needing broad capital gains tax cuts.[8] A tax break that targets human capital in this segment would promote innovative entrepreneurship without the high fiscal cost of broad capital gains tax cuts. Moreover, broad-based capital gains tax cuts do not shift capital from passive investments to private equity, unlike tax breaks on stock options and other instruments used by the VC sector.

Table 3.3 Effective tax rate on stock options in selected European countries, the U.S., and Hong Kong, 2012

Country	Tax rate, %	Country	Tax rate, %
Ireland	7.4	Finland	51.3
USA	15.0	Switzerland	51.5
Hong Kong	15.0	Spain	52.0
Netherlands	25.0	Sweden	54.3
France	29.9	Denmark	55.3
UK	28.0	Portugal	56.5
Germany	47.5	Italy	72.2
Norway	50.8		

Source Henrekson and Sanandaji (2016a)

---

[8]A mere 0.1–0.2% of all firms in the U.S. receive early-stage financing from specialized venture capitalists (Puri and Zarutskie 2012), but they constitute the majority of firms that are sufficiently successful to go public (Kaplan and Lerner 2010).

Table 3.4 Venture capital investments as a share of GDP, and the ease of getting credit in EU countries and the U.S., 2015

Country	VC investment, % of GDP	Ease of getting credit score (0–100)
USA	0.333	95.0
Denmark	0.109	70.0
Luxembourg	0.079	15.0
Finland	0.047	65.0
Ireland	0.041	70.0
Portugal	0.039	45.0
France	0.034	50.0
Sweden	0.034	55.0
Netherlands	0.033	50.0
UK	0.032	75.0
Germany	0.025	70.0
Estonia	0.023[a]	70.0
Latvia	0.023[a]	75.0
Lithuania	0.023[a]	70.0
Hungary	0.022	75.0
Belgium	0.015	45.0
Spain	0.010	60.0
Austria	0.008	60.0
Poland	0.007	75.0
Bulgaria	0.002	70.0
Czech Republic	0.002	70.0
Italy	0.002	45.0
Romania	0.001	85.0
Greece	0.000	50.0
Croatia	n/a	55.0
Cyprus	n/a	65.0
Malta	n/a	10.0
Slovakia	n/a	65.0
Slovenia	n/a	35.0

Note [a]For VC-investments, values for Estonia, Latvia and Lithuania are a Baltic average. The ranking of economies on the ease of getting credit is determined by their distance to the leading country for getting credit. These scores are the distance to frontier score for the sum of the strength of legal rights index (range 0–10); and the depth of credit information index (range 0–8). New Zealand is the leading country

Source Invest Europe (2016, p. 43) for venture capital and World Bank, *Doing Business 2016* for ease of getting credit

3.3 Regulations Governing Savings, Capital and Finance

3.3.1 Preamble

A high savings rate in a country does not guarantee the availability of financing for innovative and growth-oriented entrepreneurship, especially not in the early, precarious phase of the firm's lifecycle. In fact, some of the countries with the highest savings rates are the least entrepreneurial, whereas the United States has a notoriously low savings rate and a vibrant entrepreneurial sector. The composition of savings—not just its volume—also sways potential entrepreneurship activity in the economy. As we have already demonstrated, entrepreneurial activity hinges on accessing and raising the right kind of capital.

Numerous studies reveal that a lack of access to capital is the most significant obstacle for many business ventures (e.g., van Auken 1999 and Parker 2009). In the EU, entrepreneurs and SMEs rank financing as their second most important concern after administrative burdens (European Commission 2008), and the highly developed financial system of the United States has indeed been cited as a central reason for the emergence of its successful entrepreneurial economy (Kauffman Foundation 2007, p. 34). However, many startups do not require much capital, and financial constraints are therefore not much of a problem (Hurst and Lusardi 2004; Shane 2008, p. 79). Advances in ICT have reduced minimum capital requirements in many markets (Baumol et al. 2007, p. 236). As it stands, capital tends to constrain high-growth firms more than other firms because they often require sizable infusions of external equity to sustain growth (Baumol et al. 2007, p. 205).

Notably, the success of a startup relies on its access to equity financing, a reliance which increases (relative to debt) with the degree of risk. Ceteris paribus, small and newly established firms are more dependent on equity financing than large, well-established firms since it is more difficult for outside financiers to assess the viability and profitability of the venture. Therefore, entrepreneurial startups usually struggle to raise funds from large financial institutions and are forced to rely on insider and internal funding in their infancy. Any arrangement that channels savings and asset control to large institutional investors is therefore likely to hamper the supply of financial capital to potential entrepreneurs.

By contrast, research strongly suggests that incentives for individual wealth accumulation would likely increase entrepreneurial activity (Nykvist 2008; Parker 2009). Wealth-constrained would-be entrepreneurs are unable to forcibly signal their project's worth to outside investors by means of making sizeable equity infusions of their own. More private savings would lessen the inherent problem caused by such asymmetric information, and, if needed, enable entrepreneurs to fully finance the firm until organic growth based on retained earnings is possible. Furthermore, informal investors, such as business angels, may fill the gap between internal funding and formal VC financing (to varying degrees in different countries). Research shows that the presence of these informal investors is crucial in overcoming liquidity constraints (Ho and Wong 2007). The United Kingdom in particular has used tax relief and generous deductions to encourage business angel investments; see, e.g., Boyns et al. (2003) and Mason (2006).

Although the importance of the formal VC industry has increased over time, its presence is still rather modest in the EU (Bygrave and Hunt 2004; Lerner and Tåg 2013) with many entrepreneurial firms being too small for VC funding. However, venture capital is important for high-performing and high-growth entrepreneurial firms (Cumming 2012). It is often superior to bank finance since it also provides key expertise and access to networks that are important to entrepreneurial high-risk firms (Keuschnigg and Nielsen 2004a; Ho and Wong 2007). In this respect, it is troubling that the VC industry is less developed in Europe than in the U.S. (Bottazzi and Da Rin 2002; Da Rin et al. 2006), possibly because European business owners are less prone to accept a loss of control, which is a normal consequence of venture capital support (OECD 1998). It may be for this reason that U.S. firms grow faster than their European counterparts (Scarpetta et al. 2002; Henrekson and Sanandaji 2016a).

Appreciating the role of the VC industry in the entrepreneurial ecosystem also explains why governmental attempts to compensate for deficient private financing of innovative entrepreneurship—especially of the early-stage variety—are unlikely to be successful.[9] Any such support system must contain elements of rationing and selection in order to avoid the moral hazard problems of unmanageable proportions, and as emphasized in the discussion of targeted support in Sect. 2.2, no recipe exists that dictates how to "pick the winners" and support the right investments. By contrast, the process of evaluation in the private VC industry is highly complex and often includes tacit judgments. Granted, industry actors, despite their specialization, are at best moderately successful in picking the winners among high-risk projects (Gompers and Lerner 2004; Birch 2006; Svensson 2008; Gompers et al. 2009), but there is little empirical evidence to suggest that politically controlled organizations are better placed in this respect (Baumol et al. 2007, p. 220). Instead, such organizations might—directly or indirectly, openly or furtively, partly or completely—base their decisions on political rather than commercial criteria and therefore underperform.[10]

Moreover, decision making by business angels and VC investors is often also a matter of judgment in which the criteria are largely tacit. To have public agencies

---

[9]For example, tax revenues can be used to directly provide venture capital to the market, either through state-controlled organizations or together with private actors. In particular, governments could support the supply of early stage (seed) capital—which the formal venture capital industry typically does not provide—through public interventions.

[10]Baumol et al. (2007) assert that the Advanced Technology Program (ATP), administered by the Commerce Department in the United States, only supported ventures that also attracted private money, and there is some evidence that this has been successful. The largest U.S. program is the Small Business Innovation Research (SBIR) program. Siegel et al. (2003) conclude that both ATP and SBIR have been successful, while Lerner (2009) is more skeptical and describes many government support programs that have failed due to ill-conceived designs, incompetence among government officials and fussy goals. The only countries in which he finds that government support schemes have been a definite success are Singapore and Israel.

use similar criteria does not mesh with the requirement of treating all citizens equally under the law. Finally, failure is an inherent part of entrepreneurship, and private investors consciously assume such risk. It is more difficult for elected politicians who handle taxpayers' money to motivate such risk-taking and the inevitable losses in numerous projects.

3.3.2 Reform Agenda

As a long-term solution, the best way to ensure the financing of entrepreneurial firms is likely to be the pursuit of policies that encourage private wealth accumulation in forms that do not preclude the assets from being used as equity in entrepreneurial ventures.[11] However, there is currently a strong tendency to introduce or increase the use of funded pension systems both in the private and public sectors, and there is little reason to believe that this trend will be reversed. In Sweden, for example, collectively agreed supplementary pension schemes cover virtually all tenured employees with payments into those systems amounting to approximately 10% of taxable labor income (Riksbanken 2014; Svensk Försäkring 2015).[12] Total assets amount to some two-thirds of Swedish GDP and 130% of household disposable income. Aggregate pension fund assets as a share of GDP are especially large in the United Kingdom and the Netherlands, but they are also high in Ireland, Finland and Denmark, while they are still small in the Eastern European countries and in Germany, France and Italy (OECD 2015b).

Since a progressively larger share of savings goes into pension funds,[13] there is a growing need for at least part of these assets to be invested in entrepreneurial firms and not just in real estate, public stocks and high-rated bonds. Since large financial institutions can rarely invest directly in small and new firms, a bridging intermediating role must be provided by a professional VC sector, as discussed in Sect. 3.3.1. As revealed in the first column of Table 3.4,[14] the differences here are substantial across Europe, with Denmark and Luxembourg clearly leading, whereas the Eastern European and the Mediterranean countries for which there are data are located at the bottom.

Here, policymakers could be inspired by the U.S. experience of the 1970s and 1980s, and adopt a broad-based policy approach: an encouraging legal framework that combines tax cuts in capital gains with legislation allowing pension funds to

---

[11]Pelikan (1988) provides forceful arguments supporting this view.

[12]Marginal payments are at least 38% on the part of wages, which only slightly exceeds the average wage for full-time workers (including a tax of 24% on collectively agreed pension premiums).

[13]See Ebbinghaus (2011) regarding the trend away from pay-as-you-go and towards the privatization of pension systems in Europe.

[14]Hong Kong and Norway are not included in Table 3.4. According to Lerner and Tåg (2013), the sizes of their VC sectors were 0.23 and 0.053% of GDP, respectively.

invest in high-risk securities issued by small and new firms as well as VC funds (Gompers and Lerner 1999; cf. Keuschnigg and Nielsen 2004a, b). Additionally, as discussed in Sect. 3.2, effective tax treatments of options contracts are necessary to enable VC firms and other actors in the entrepreneurial ecosystem to design the appropriate incentive contracts for founders and other key personnel needed to build innovative firms (Henrekson and Rosenberg 2001). Without such opportunities, a sizeable and efficient VC sector cannot develop.

By contrast, debt financing is unlikely to be a viable alternative to external equity investments in the early entrepreneurial phase since such financing presupposes positive cash flows and low risk ventures—meaning that innovative entrepreneurship is not favored compared to activities with low risk and assets that can be collateralized. A comparison of the first and second column of Table 3.4 reveals that many of the countries with low scores on the size of external equity investment activity rank highly regarding the ease of getting credit (e.g., Romania, Hungary and Bulgaria). While some economies have traditionally been characterized as bank-centered—Germany being the archetypical case—this has changed profoundly over the last two decades. Bank lending is no longer a viable option for financing high-risk innovative entrepreneurship that does not occur within the boundaries of large firms. Thus, bank financing and monitoring is not a viable alternative to institutional reform that would pave the way for external equity investment.

Moreover, it is important to recognize that venture capitalists and other early-phase equity investors only are ownership specialists up to a certain point in the entrepreneurial ecosystem, since a highly successful entrepreneurial firm will reach a point at which it may be appropriate to sell the firm. That said, the existence of a viable market for corporate control later in the firm lifecycle matters for early-stage entrepreneurs, since this market affects the expected future value of embarking on an entrepreneurial venture (Norbäck and Persson 2009, 2012).

There are three principal ways in which an entrepreneurial exit can be done. The first is through a trade sale, i.e., being acquired by an incumbent firm that wants to gain access to new technologies and innovation (or just eliminate a future competitor), which is quite common in countries such as the Netherlands. The second way is by going public through an IPO, which is possible if there is a sizeable public stock market. The third way is by turning to buyout firms (the secondary market equivalent of VC firms). This option is contingent on the existence of a buyout sector through which pension savings can be channeled to the business sector in the form of equity investment. As shown in Table 3.5, there are large cross-country differences in the size of public stock markets and buyout sectors. These sectors are generally small in countries with small VC sectors and vice versa. Hence, they are quite large in the Anglo-Saxon countries, the Nordic countries, and the Netherlands, but small in Eastern Europe and the Mediterranean countries. This hints at strong complementarities between the early- and late-stage vehicles for corporate control and prompts us to look for underlying causes of the absence of these markets.

Table 3.5 Buyout investment and market capitalization as a percentage of GDP in EU countries and the U.S., 2015

Country	Buyout investment	Market capitalization
USA	3.49	151.2
UK	0.68	106.5
Sweden	0.32	135.2
Denmark	0.31	71.3 (2012)
France	0.31	73.7
Finland	0.18	81.8
Netherlands	0.16	89.5
Germany	0.15	44.9
Poland	0.15	31.0
Belgium	0.14	71.2
Hungary	0.087	10.5
Luxembourg	0.062	97.4
Spain	0.062	71.9
Italy	0.060	21.8 (2008)
Ireland	0.030	57.2
Romania	0.029	11.2
Bulgaria	0.024	9.7
Portugal	0.023	25.1
Estonia	0.013[a]	10.1 (2012)
Latvia	0.013[a]	4.0 (2012)
Lithuania	0.013[a]	9.3 (2012)
Austria	0.008	22.2
Czech Republic	0.000	36.5 (2007)
Greece	0.000	23.4
Croatia		38.6 (2013)
Cyprus		17.4
Malta		44.1 (2013)
Slovakia		4.9
Slovenia		15.2

Note [a]For buyout investment, values for Estonia, Latvia and Lithuania are a Baltic average. Market capitalization is the share price times the number of shares outstanding. Listed domestic companies are the domestically incorporated companies listed on the country's stock exchanges at the end of the year. Listed companies do not include investment companies, mutual funds, or other collective investment vehicles. Data are missing for some of the EU countries

Source For buyout: Invest Europe (2016, p. 44) for EU countries and American Investment Council and World Bank for the U.S. For market capitalization: World Federation of Exchanges database; extracted from the World Bank's World Development Indicators database (2006–14) for all countries except for Sweden, Finland and Denmark. Source Denmark: "World Development Indicators 2014". Source Sweden: Riksbanken and Statistics Sweden. Source Finland: Finlands Bank and Statistikcentralen

One likely reason for small public stock markets is the weak protection of minority investors, but a more fundamental reason for underdevelopment in each of these areas is probably weak property rights protection, discussed in Sect. 3.1 (Levine 2005). Without such protection, no actors are likely to have sufficient incentives to take the risks required for successful corporate control and guidance at any stage of the firm lifecycle unless that agent has total control and owns 100% of the equity. Under such circumstances, pension savings and other institutional capital would be barred from access to ownership stakes in the corporate sector.

3.4 The Organization of Labor Markets and Social Insurance Systems

3.4.1 Preamble

Legislation and regulations pertaining to labor markets and wage setting influence incentives for entrepreneurship since contracting freedom becomes constrained. It therefore curtails possible combinations of factors of production and the best use of the various functions in the skill structure, notably those related to competent employees. Labor security mandates fall more heavily on younger, smaller, and less capital-intensive employers—categories in which entrepreneurial firms are over-represented. Severance pay and strict regulations governing the order of dismissal in the case of redundancy are factors that keep entrepreneurs from adjusting their workforce in response to market fluctuations and changes in required skills, thereby increasing the risk of their projects (Audretsch et al. 2002). Such lack of flexibility may become detrimental to the overall economy, making it less adaptable to changes. In addition, labor market regulation can influence entrepreneurial activity by affecting the relative advantage of being an employee; far-reaching employment protection legislation increases an employee's opportunity cost of changing employers or leaving a secure salaried job to become self-employed (Ho and Wong 2007; van Stel et al. 2007).

Less stringent legislation for temporary employment contracts would enable an important channel for job creation. However, from the ecosystem perspective, this is a second-best solution since staff on temporary contracts will be less motivated to invest in firm-specific skills and commit less strongly to the firm than employees on permanent contracts.[15] Thus, it becomes less likely that the firm will be able to attract workers who have highly valued skills or are inclined to develop such skills. Hence, a large discrepancy in the degree of protection between permanent and

---

[15]*Prima facie*, one may infer that permanent contracts are of little value in high-risk entrepreneurial ventures, as the contract is not secure anyway. However, unless the firm offers a permanent contract, the employee runs the risk of being dismissed when the temporary contract expires even if the venture is successful.

temporary contracts offers a comparative advantage to low-skill industries in which employees are highly substitutable. Such industries tend to be less innovative and have lower productivity.

Research has found that labor market regulations shape the level of nascent entrepreneurship more than differences in entry regulations, with the result that entrepreneurship is higher in countries in which hiring and dismissing employees is relatively easy and inexpensive (Niehof 1999; OECD 2003; van Stel et al. 2007). In addition, labor market deregulation can and has stimulated entrepreneurial activity in many OECD countries (OECD 1998, 2000). Europe's stricter employment protection legislation may partly explain its lower frequency of new, rapidly growing firms relative to the United States (Baumol et al. 2007, p. 210 and 222).[16]

The social security system is closely linked to the regime governing the labor market. Public income insurance systems in combination with strict labor security legislation tend to penalize individuals who assume entrepreneurial risk (Ilmakunnas and Kanniainen 2001). This is because these systems confer a relative advantage on employees with many social security benefits—such as disability, sickness, unemployment and pension benefits—being explicitly linked to formal employment. These benefits further increase the opportunity cost of leaving a tenured position as an employee and thus reduce the incentives for entrepreneurship (Audretsch et al. 2002).

Many are unwilling to forgo a large part of their social protection in exchange for an uncertain and volatile entrepreneurial income. Making parts of social insurance benefits "portable"—e.g., by decoupling health insurance—between jobs and between regular employment and self-employment would mitigate this effect. However, even if it were possible to "generalize" the social security system, the self-employed and owners/managers of small entrepreneurial firms would still be unable to make practical use of the full extent of the system's benefits, such as those related to parental or sick leave.

Generous unemployment benefits naturally discourage the unemployed from becoming self-employed, and in countries in which the unemployed receive a high proportion of their former wage, the rate of new firm formation is lower (Nickell 1997; Delmar et al. 2005; Koellinger and Minniti 2009). However, as already noted in Sect. 2.1, going from unemployment to self-employment is oftentimes a form of necessity entrepreneurship, which is unlikely to have many positive economic effects.

---

[16]Stringent labor market regulations thus deter and impede business activities but may simultaneously boost self-employment due to evasive measures. To circumvent stringent regulations, potential entrepreneurs can choose to become self-employed themselves. They could also decide to eschew hiring employees in favor of cooperating in networks with other self-employed individuals since no labor security is mandated for the self-employed and compensation and working hours are unregulated. However, this type of self-employment should not be interpreted as a sign of entrepreneurial dynamism but instead as a costly, albeit necessary, strategy to evade onerous regulation. Part of the increase in self-employment in recent years in many highly regulated economies is likely driven by such considerations (Liebregts 2016).

3.4.2   Reform Agenda

3.4.2.1   Employment Protection Legislation

Figure 3.2 shows the stringency of employment protection legislation (EPL) in the EU countries and in the United States for temporary contracts (y-axis) and permanent contracts (x-axis). The two measures reveal considerable positive correlation ($r = 0.46$). The Anglo-Saxon countries stand out as having the least stringent EPL by far, even though most other countries have liberalized their legislation for permanent employment in recent decades (Skedinger 2010; Martin and Scarpetta 2012). For temporary contracts, Sweden and Germany stand out for their substantial liberalization over the past 20 years; notably, these are two of the top-performing EU countries in terms of employment (see Fig. 2.2). They also rank among the countries with the highest share of temporary employment. In Sweden, as much as 56% of employed 15–24-year-olds were on temporary contracts in 2015 (OECD 2016).

The Mediterranean countries (Portugal, Italy, Spain and Greece) have also liberalized their temporary employment legislation, and even though it remains comparatively stringent, the share of employed 15–24-year olds on temporary contracts is above 50% in all those nations except Greece (OECD 2016). By

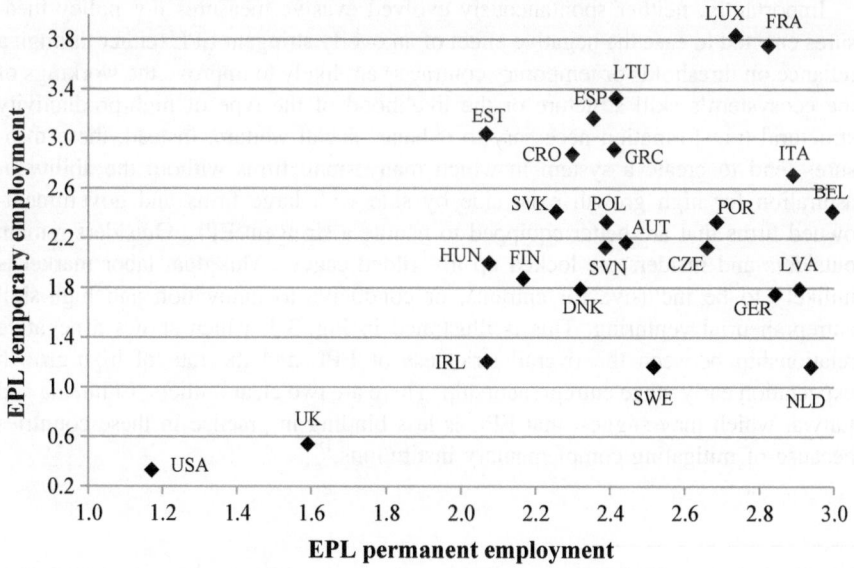

Fig. 3.2 Stringency of employment protection legislation for workers on permanent and temporary contracts in EU countries and the U.S., 2013. *Note* The scale of the index is 0–6, where 6 represents the most stringent regulation. 2013 is the latest available year. The index for permanent employment is the index for individual and permanent dismissals. *Source* OECD/IAB Employment Protection Database, 2013 update

contrast, all Eastern European countries have increased the stringency of their legislation related to temporary contracts, which is noteworthy given their generally weak employment performance. Overall, legislation with respect to both types of contracts remains quite strict in most Mediterranean and Continental European countries.

Policymakers in several European countries are aware that the EPL may be too stringent; to mitigate the negative effect, they have instituted firm-size thresholds below which labor regulations are less onerous. Again, such a policy of exceptions can be criticized on neutrality grounds since, in practice, this is the equivalent of a tax on firm growth. Indeed, it has been revealed that firms are reluctant to grow beyond the size threshold in Germany (Autio et al. 2007), France (Garicano et al. 2016), Portugal (Braguinsky et al. 2011), and Italy (Schivardi and Torrini 2008).[17] Thus, firms are incentivized to remain small, and many entrepreneurs will never discover that they could have become high-impact entrepreneurs because they do not even try. That said, stringent employment regulations may create strong incentives for actors in the skill structure to devise arrangements to circumvent the regulations. Important symptoms of such attempts to create flexibility in several European countries include increased self-employment, the emergence of an underground economy in which the government does not or cannot enforce regulations, and an increased reliance on temporary employment. Additionally, firms may remain small to avoid unionization and the obligation to sign collective agreements, thus benefitting from greater freedom of contracting.

Importantly, neither spontaneously evolved evasive measures nor policy measures enacted to ease the negative effect of an overly stringent EPL (either through a reliance on thresholds or temporary contracts) are likely to improve the workings of the ecosystem's skill structure or the likelihood of the type of high-productivity structural transformation necessary to enhance social welfare. Instead, these measures tend to create a system in which many small firms without the ability or aspiration for high growth exist side by side with large firms and government-owned firms that are better equipped to handle a stringent EPL. Outsiders remain outsiders and insiders are locked up in "gilded cages". This dual labor market is unlikely to be inclusive for entrants, or conducive to innovation and high-skill entrepreneurial venturing. This is illustrated in Fig. 3.3, which shows a negative relationship between the overall strictness of EPL and the rate of high-growth expectation early-stage entrepreneurship. There are two clear outliers, Lithuania and Latvia, which may suggest that EPL is less binding in practice in these countries because of mitigating complementary institutions.[18]

---

[17]In Germany, the administrative cost based on the design of the regulatory framework rises sharply for firms with 50 employees or more. When French firms reach 50 employees, they must form work councils, provide more union representation and face higher firing costs. Portugal and Italy have important regulatory limits already at 15 employees with similar growth-impeding effects.

[18]$r = -0.43$ if Latvia and Lithuania are excluded, otherwise $r = -0.31$.

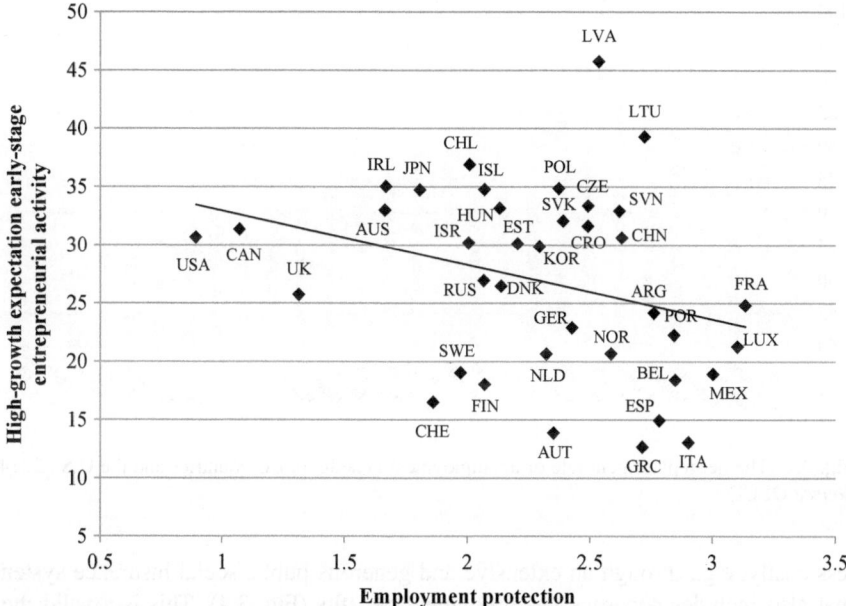

Fig. 3.3 The strictness of employment protection and high-growth expectation early-stage entrepreneurial activity, 2010–13. *Note* Both variables are averaged over the four years 2010–13. Permanent EPL is given a weight of 2/3 and temporary EPL a weight of 1/3. *Source* Global Entrepreneurship Monitor and OECD/IAB Employment Protection Database, 2013 update

If the goal is to make the European Union more inclusive, innovative and entrepreneurial, it is highly advisable that the most regulated countries reduce the stringency of their EPL for permanent contracts. A competently implemented liberalization will reduce job security but increase employment security for workers, as labor demand will increase and more opportunities will be created in the labor market. That said, the impact and strictness of employment protection legislation depends on a complex combination of components, such as grounds for individual dismissal, redundancy procedures, mandated periods of advanced notice, severance payments, special requirements for collective dismissals, rules favoring disadvantaged groups, and so forth. For liberalization to have the desired results, countries must develop their own strategies to avoid jeopardizing the process, ideally by considering and possibly emulating the paths already taken by similar countries. This also presupposes the implementation of complementary social insurance institutions.

3.4.2.2   Social Insurance Systems

In principle, providing insurance for unfavorable outcomes can encourage individuals to pursue entrepreneurial endeavors by making the burden of uncertainty

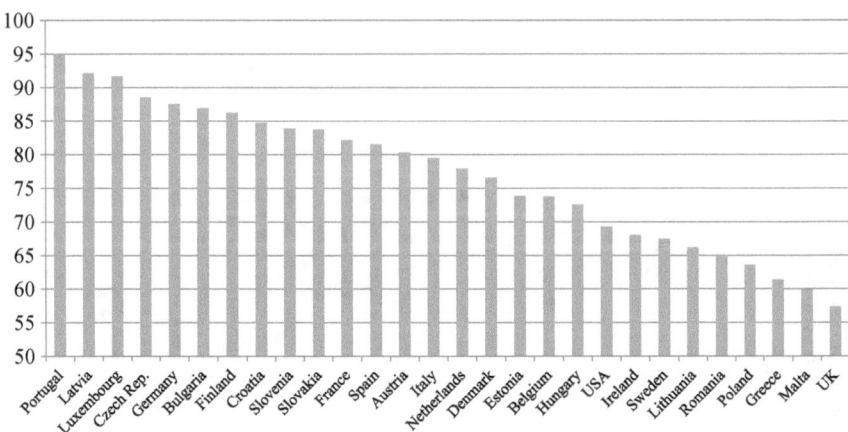

Fig. 3.4 The net replacement rate of unemployment benefits in EU countries and the U.S., 2014. *Source* OECD

less costly, e.g., through an extensive and generous public social insurance system that also includes generous unemployment benefits (Fig. 3.4). This is a valid theoretical point shown formally by Sinn (1996), but it is an open question as to whether it is empirically important. Furthermore, the point no longer holds in labor markets in which job security is closely linked to job tenure; ultimately, what matters is the opportunity cost, i.e., how much an employee must sacrifice in terms of income and security if he or she transfers to self-employment or a risky job in an entrepreneurial firm.

For a tenured employee with a low-risk employer, the opportunity cost is high in many countries in which important benefits are tied to employment. Company-specific health insurance is an obvious example of such a benefit; another is accumulated pension assets, which may be difficult to transfer when switching employer and/or industry. To the extent that this is true, the mobility of (especially older) workers across firms is hampered, and the hiring of the elderly unemployed is discouraged.[19] Decoupling these and other benefits from employment would increase labor flexibility and lessen the risk that workers and potential entrepreneurs become "trapped" in large companies by reducing fears of losing adequate health insurance and other important employment benefits. In addition, supplementary pension plans should be made fully actuarial and portable. Making social security more portable and tied to the individual would also improve the low geographical

---

[19]Supplementary pension plans that are not fully actuarial and individualized often contain elements of redistribution and risk-sharing across individuals in a group, like white-collar workers in a certain industry. In addition, the pension benefit level is often disproportionately tied to the wage level achieved towards the end of an employee's professional career, making elderly employees unwilling to change to lower paid jobs even if that would mean that their career would be prolonged and the final retirement age would be deferred.

mobility of workers in Europe, since being tied to a job in a firm also implies being tied to a specific location.

In this manner, public welfare systems can also reduce the need for stringent and costly employment protection legislation by replacing mandated security at the firm level, something which would arguably increase the acceptance of labor market liberalizations in many EU countries. An important role model in this respect is the *flexicurity* system of Denmark in which generous welfare protection and opportunities for retraining are combined with weak job security mandates (Andersen 2005). By contrast, a Swedish employee who voluntarily gives up a tenured position for self-employment may ultimately have no more security than what is provided by (means-tested) social welfare; in effect, the public income insurance systems and the employment security legislation tend to penalize individuals who assume entrepreneurial risk. Thus, the opportunity cost of giving up a tenured position in Denmark is substantially lower than in Sweden.

While the specifics can and will vary, we can infer that an important component of a policy that makes society more innovative and entrepreneurial involves making the individual's social insurances as portable as possible when changing jobs and moving between salaried employment and self-employment. This should be the case regardless of whether the insurance is public, paid by the individual herself, or paid by the employer based on individual or collective (union) agreement. One example of how to achieve this portability is the Austrian reform of 2003, which converted uncertain firing costs for employers into a system of individual savings accounts, funded by an employer-paid payroll tax (Hofer 2007). This system guarantees the employer certainty about the cost of any future dismissal when a person is first hired, while workers do not lose their entitlement to severance pay should they quit to take a new job.

At the same time, an efficient flexicurity model must encourage the retraining of redundant workers, possibly in the dual sense that training should be supplied and that people should be obliged to accept it to draw unemployment benefits. Yet for the model to function properly, unemployment benefits cannot be so high that they reduce incentives for future job search for workers who become unemployed. Figure 3.4 reveals considerable variation in the net replacement rate of unemployment benefits across European countries. The incentive effects of a certain replacement rate depend on other complementary rules and institutions, particularly the maximum number of days during which benefits can be received, the scope for declining job offers and retraining programs, and whether the recipient can be obligated to accept a job offer even if that entails moving to another location or commuting long distances.

3.4.2.3 Conclusions on the Organization of Labor Markets

The most important channel by which labor market institutions affect entrepreneurship is through their influence on the supply of skilled workers. Given the large worker flows required in a dynamic entrepreneurial ecosystem, institutions should facilitate the recruitment of workers with the necessary competencies. Here, as we have seen, several institutional complementarities come into play. Importantly, this requires the removal of onerous employment protection legislation, as this discourages potential high-growth firms from expanding. Furthermore, social security institutions should enable the portability of tenure rights and pension plans, as well as a full decoupling of health insurance from the current employer. It should be stressed that to be as efficient as possible, these reforms should not be made in isolation but as part of a comprehensive reform package that also includes other areas, especially tax policy and competition policy, as discussed in Sects. 3.2 and 3.5.

3.5 Regulation of Goods and Service Markets

3.5.1 Preamble

Natural entry barriers such as scale economies and capital requirements affect the workings of the actors in the ecosystem's skill structure, but artificial barriers created by governments are also important factors when considering the ease of starting a business (Begley et al. 2005; Dana 1990; Djankov and Murrell 2002). While environmental, health and safety regulations are often well motivated, competition policies that rely on excessive rules and procedures may discourage potential entrepreneurs (Dana 1990; Gnyawali and Fogel 1994; Djankov et al. 2003; Begley et al. 2005) and hamper the process of creative destruction (La Porta et al. 1997; Caballero and Hammour 2000; Desai et al. 2003).

Arguably, most damaging are restrictions and prohibitions against entry into certain sectors of the economy (such as health care) as well as administrative costs and regulatory burdens imposed on new and/or existing firms. Granted, some governmental entry barriers can be justified as consumer protection against fraudulent or incompetent business owners, and few would support a system in which anybody could work as a doctor, surgeon, or psychologist (OECD 2007). However, occupational licensing becomes problematic when it results in unjustified profit opportunities for license holders rather than consumer protection. Consequently, licensing and other overly extensive regulations may curb the rate of innovation and hamper productive entrepreneurship (Kleiner 2006). Today, Europe has over 5,000 regulated professions involving over 50 million people, and according to the European Commission (2015, p. 7): "many of these regulations are now disproportionate and create unnecessary regulatory obstacles to the mobility of professionals, lowering productivity" (cf. Erixon and Weigel 2016).

In recent decades, governments of developed countries have deregulated product markets with the aim of increasing market contestability and providing more opportunities for private entrepreneurship within sectors such as telecommunications, energy production, transportation, and financial services. The scope for new high-impact entrepreneurship has thus increased dramatically. Furthermore, welfare states increasingly recognize that ensuring access to health care and other social goods and services does not necessarily require the government to produce such goods. The Dutch example reveals that it may even be possible to eschew public financing: In the Netherlands, health care insurance is fully privatized in the sense that all private suppliers are forced to offer a standardized policy at a (competitive) price, while all citizens are forced to buy such a policy (Schäfer et al. 2010).

Overall, governments are increasingly utilizing market-type mechanisms[20] that combine private provision and public financing of these services, such as outsourcing, vouchers and public–private partnerships. In many instances, opening previously monopolized markets to private providers has led to impressive entrepreneurial performances, hinting at a largely untapped productive potential in sectors such as health care, education, and care of children and the elderly. As examples, consider the voucher system for school choice that was introduced in Sweden in the early 1990s and the (contemporaneous) outsourcing of health care by many local and regional governments, which paved the way for several high-growth firms, some of which have since become multinationals.[21] Andersson and Jordahl (2013) survey the empirical literature on the effect of outsourcing public services and conclude that it generally reduces costs without hurting quality. This is clearly the case for "perfectly contractible services" such as garbage collection, but outsourcing also often seems to work reasonably well for services with more difficult contracting problems, e.g., fire protection and prisons. However, outsourcing seems to be more problematic for credence goods, that is, goods for which buyers have a hard time determining the total cost and benefit even after purchase and use (Emons 1997), which is the case for many social services, such as education and medical treatments.[22]

Welfare services are complex and difficult to procure regardless of the source of financing. When under the public domain, complexities arise from several additional sources: formalized procurement processes are likely to favor large actors and curb competition; producers cannot charge extra for quality improvements; costly excess capacity may arise; a lack of information makes rational decision making difficult for users; evaluations and compliance control are skill- and resource-intensive; segregating forces exist; and individual users and suppliers do not consider how society is affected.

---

[20]OECD (2005, p. 130) defines a market-type mechanism as "encompassing all arrangements where at least one significant characteristic of markets is present."

[21]One of the most well-known examples is the health care provider Capio, which was founded in Sweden in 1994. In 2016, Capio had 12,500 employees in four countries. There are also several large operators in elderly care, and they are gradually becoming multinational as well. The largest of these firms, Attendo, had roughly 15,000 employees in late 2016.

[22]This fact makes these goods more susceptible to fraud and manipulation. See Nooteboom (2014) for an in-depth discussion of the many challenges involved. Thus far, there are few studies comparing the quality of services produced by for-profit firms and by government providers, although the evidence so far rather shows that the for-profit firms offer higher quality (Bergman et al. 2016).

In these sensitive areas, considerations of public interest should move firms beyond what the law demands and towards what is really in their long-term interest. The challenge is to create what Kay (2004) calls "embedded markets" in which governments participate without controlling, financial incentives exist but do not dominate, pluralist structures can evolve based on experimentation, and social norms continue to play a key role in maintaining compliance with a system that inspires pride in the inhabitants. Of course, this necessitates that the agents involved "take upon themselves a wider set of responsibilities" (Kay 2004, p. 344).

Market regulations incentivizing actors in the skill structure to innovate and experiment to the greatest possible extent are essential for a well-functioning entrepreneurial ecosystem. Market-leading incumbents should not be allowed to unduly exploit their dominant market positions, and all markets should be as contestable as possible. However, drafting appropriately balanced regulations is easier said than done; examples abound of the regulatory framework favoring a certain interest group rather than the general public interest (Stigler 1971; Wagner 2014), giving rise to large fixed costs that effectively bar smaller actors from entering the market (Begley et al. 2005) or falling short of its objectives in other ways. Technological change may also turn regulations into obsolete constraints at best and barriers to new entrants at worst, rendering adaptations to changing conditions more difficult.

The fact that a certain market is formally deregulated does not guarantee contestability. There can still be artificial barriers created by governments and excessive rules and procedures that discourage entrepreneurial entrants from challenging incumbents,[23] which hampers the process of structural change and creative destruction. Thus, for market competition to work efficiently, it must be easy to start a business.

3.5.2   Reform Agenda

Figure 3.5 reveals how the EU countries compare with respect to the ease of starting a business relative to the United States and New Zealand, which is the leading country. Countries such as Germany, Austria and Malta show considerable room for improvement, while the western EU countries have high overall scores on this measure. Apart from Poland and the Czech Republic, this is also the case for the Eastern European countries.

The picture that emerges from Fig. 3.5 appears fairly bright. Part of the explanation can be traced to the wave of product market deregulation that began in the United States around 1980 and then quickly spread to other countries, rekindling

---

[23]Formal and informal institutions tend to serve the economic status quo, conserving old habits and incumbent economic interests (Elert and Henrekson 2017). This tendency is often reinforced by attempts by large corporations and other incumbent interests to shape government regulations in ways that are favorable to them (Battilana et al. 2009; Lawton et al. 2013).

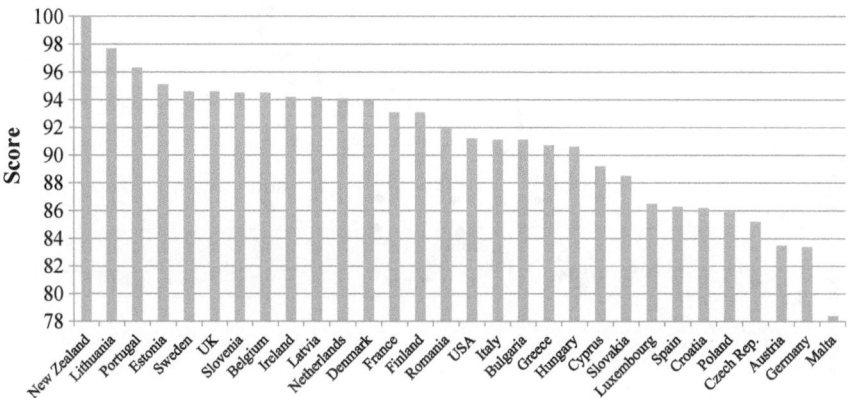

Fig. 3.5 Ease of starting a business in EU countries, the U.S., and the leading country (New Zealand), 2015. *Note* The ranking of economies on the ease of starting a business is determined based on their distance to frontier scores for starting a business. These scores are the simple average of the distance to frontier scores for each of the component indicators. *Source* World Bank, *Ease of Doing Business Index 2016*

innovation and entrepreneurship after a decade of stagflation and recurrent structural crises (Audretsch and Thurik 2000). Product market reform is also a prime ingredient of the European integration effort; having similar product market regulations in all EU countries is considered necessary by European policymakers to fulfill the vision of transforming the European Union into one single market.

Nevertheless, as seen in Fig. 3.6, which presents the strictness of product and service market regulations in the EU and the United States, countries still exhibit large differences in the extent of their product market regulations in the European Union despite several rounds of product market deregulations. The differences are even larger in regard to service sector regulations (measured on the vertical axis), and the two measures are strongly correlated; countries with highly regulated product markets tend to have strictly regulated service markets and vice versa ($r = 0.70$). Furthermore, Western European countries generally score better than Eastern European and Mediterranean countries.

Interestingly, however, no similar correspondence can be observed between these two indices and the measure of the ease of starting a business (Table 3.6). This suggests that complementarities with factors besides regulations of these markets could affect the perceived possibility of starting a business. For example, the fact that Austria and Germany score poorly in terms of the ease of starting a business despite their relaxed product and service market regulations could be because a great deal more is involved in setting up a firm than just product market regulations, including taxes, red tape, and conditions for financing.

Service sectors are particularly important for' the future of the entrepreneurial ecosystem for multiple reasons. First, they have a highly income-elastic demand and hold possibly the greatest future potential for entrepreneurship. If onerous regulations limit that potential, the consequence can be highly detrimental for the

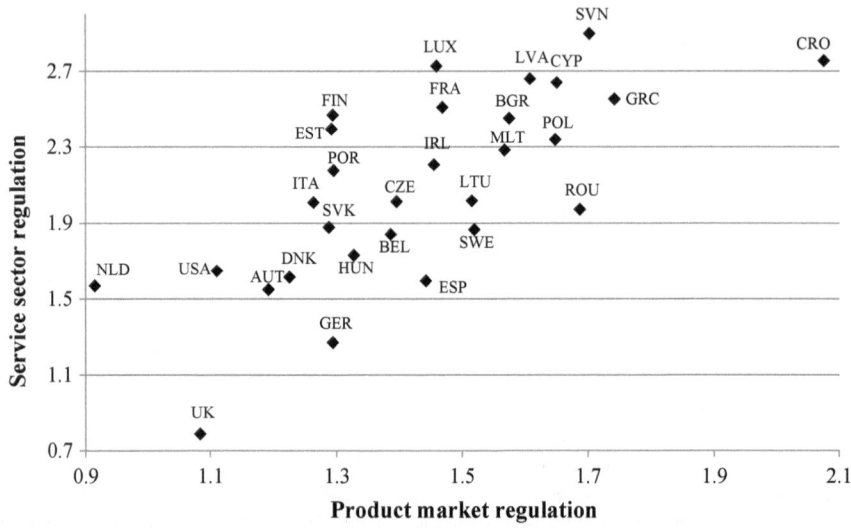

Fig. 3.6 Strictness of product and service market regulations in EU countries and the U.S., 2013. *Note* The scale of the index is 0–6, where a larger number means a more stringent regulation. 2013 is the latest available year. The product market regulation index is OECD's aggregate indicator; the service sector index is the arithmetic average of the OECD indices for professional services, retail trade and the network sectors (transportation, energy, telecom and mail). The indices are based on responses of national governments to the OECD Regulatory Indicator Questionnaires. *Source* OECD, *Product Market Regulation Database*

Table 3.6 The correlations between the ease of starting a business and the strictness of product (PMR) and service market regulations (SMR)

	PMR	SMR	Ease of starting
PMR	1.00		
SMR	0.70*	1.00	
Ease of starting	−0.19	0.02	1.00

Note *denotes statistical significance at the 1% level
Source OECD, *Product Market Regulation Database* for PMR and SMR, and World Bank, *Ease of Doing Business Index 2016*

economy as a whole.[24] Second, as already noted, it is becoming increasingly clear that ensuring access to health care and other social goods and services does not necessarily require government production of such goods, and as the Dutch case shows, it may not even require direct public financing (although that is likely to remain the default option in most EU countries for historical reasons). Hence, deregulation of services promises to open entirely new arenas for private innovation and entrepreneurial venturing.

---

[24]According to studies on the U.S., the income elasticity for health care and education is approximately 1.6 (Fogel 1999).

Perhaps most importantly, to tap the potential and handle the challenge of this combination of public financing and private production, novel institutional arrangements and experimentation are necessary to address the challenging fact that consumers do not pay producers directly. Manipulation and a wasteful use of resources are more likely to occur when the state acts as intermediary for an anonymous and absent third party (the taxpayers) and finances transactions between the producer and the consumer even if there is freedom of choice and competition.[25] Providers typically have limited options to offer and charge for extra quality added to what is granted through the tax-financed system. Consequently, customers will be barred from buying their preferred qualities and quantities of services from their preferred providers, and there will not be any signaling from spending decisions by demanding customers.

Unless governments experiment and innovate regarding the design of the regulatory framework governing activities characterized by a mixture of private production and public financing, the full benefits of innovation and entrepreneurial initiatives cannot be reaped, and the ecosystem's skill structure will remain incomplete. Allowing private for-profit firms in these areas is also the most important channel through which pension savings (to a considerable extent via private equity firms) can be used to innovate and build capacity in the primarily tax-financed social service sectors.

3.6 Bankruptcy Law and Insolvency Regulation

3.6.1 Preamble

The entrepreneurial ecosystem is experimental at its core. Failure is therefore a signal of paramount importance to the actors in the skill structure. If the economy is to evolve and develop, unsuccessful and unproductive entrepreneurial ventures must close down, so that their resources can be redirected to more productive uses. All failed projects should not be considered a waste of resources, and bankruptcies are neither unproductive nor destructive; instead, the failure of a firm provides valuable information to other economic agents about whether an endeavor is profitable. Moreover, the knowledge from failed projects and ideas can often be recycled and improved either in a restructured venture with new management or in a different firm. Past failure can thereby be part of the foundation for future success. The restriction or delay of this process by stringent bankruptcy regulation harms knowledge generation and development (Holbrook et al. 2000; Gilbert et al. 2004; Armour and Cummings 2008).

---

[25]Welfare services are supplied and consumed in so-called quasi-markets that are characterized by a series of problems that must be addressed. Le Grand and Bartlett (1993) present a theoretical analysis of quasi-markets.

Psychological costs often accompany bankruptcies, and in many countries, the public exhibits negative attitudes towards business failures (OECD 1998; Eberhart et al. 2017), which are stigmas that may unnecessarily discourage people from entrepreneurial activities. Some countries, such as the United States, look more favorably upon failed business projects (Audretsch et al. 2002), and it is important that the business culture gives failed entrepreneurs a "second chance" and allows them to start anew. Empirical research also shows that so-called habitual or serial entrepreneurs are more successful (Ucbasaran et al. 2008)—re-starters often possess valuable experience and business connections that increase their probability of success in the future. It is imperative that formal and informal institutions do not inhibit failed entrepreneurs' willingness to try new projects.

Meanwhile, from the perspective of the potential entrepreneur, stringent bankruptcy laws are discouraging because they add to the perceived cost of starting a business. Any new business can fail, and processes of business formation, selection, and destruction often include a positive information and knowledge externality that the potential entrepreneur does not consider when starting a business. Relatively generous bankruptcy laws and insolvency regulations therefore seem reasonable with provision for discharge clauses, the postponement of debt service and repayment, and the possibility of restructuring.

3.6.2 Reform Agenda

An efficient handling of ailing firms calls for a well-designed and effective bankruptcy law and insolvency regulation to do the following: (i) minimize the time and costs to society in phasing out unprofitable and inefficient firms such that resources can be reallocated to more efficient uses, and (ii) minimize the damages for other parties involved, such as creditors, customers, suppliers, employees and the government. However, not all insolvent firms should be closed. A firm is insolvent when the value of its assets is less than its debt and when it is unable to repay its outstanding debt, but a firm may simply be experiencing temporary financial difficulties. If so, the best solution for both the firm and its creditors is normally firm restructuring and debt reduction (a "haircut") through negotiations with the firm's creditors.

On the one hand, it should not be too easy to file for bankruptcy. If writing off debt and starting anew is too convenient a resort for failing entrepreneurs, it may encourage exploitation and destructive entrepreneurship, harming creditors and the rest of society (OECD 1998; Audretsch et al. 2002). On the other hand, a person who goes bankrupt because of a failed venture should not automatically be stigmatized and forever ostracized from future entrepreneurship.

In essence, the insolvency regulation should strive to protect inherently healthy and promising ventures. If they are too hastily shut down, with their remaining assets shifted out to creditors, the result may very well be excessive value destruction. If the operation itself is healthy, it is often sufficient that the current

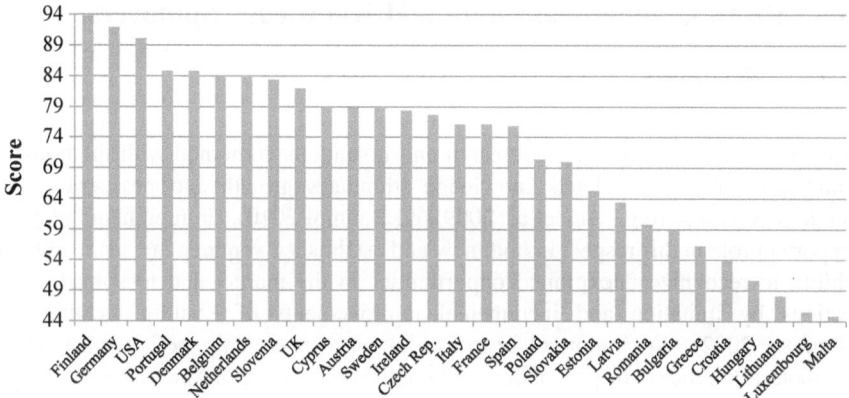

Fig. 3.7 Ease of resolving insolvency in EU countries and the U.S., 2015. *Note* The ranking of economies on the ease of resolving insolvency is determined based on their distance to frontier scores for resolving insolvency. These scores are the simple average of the distance to frontier scores for the recovery rate and the strength of insolvency framework index. Finland is also the most highly ranked country in the world. *Source* World Bank, *Doing Business 2016*

owners lose all their equity, that the debt is restructured and that the consortium of debtors find a new controlling owner after restructuring (Becker and Josephson 2016).

As shown in Fig. 3.7, there are substantial differences among the EU countries with regard to the ease of resolving insolvency. Finland and Germany are thought to have the best regulatory framework in this respect—even better than that of the United States—and the rest of Western Europe also scores high except for Luxembourg. Meanwhile, the Eastern European and Mediterranean countries rank low with Portugal, Slovenia and Cyprus as interesting exceptions.

While laggard countries must improve their insolvency regulation in order to become more innovative and entrepreneurial, this cannot be done in isolation. Reforms in this direction have to be combined with a strengthening of the rule of law and the security of property rights; otherwise, the reforms may prove ineffective or even facilitate abuse and fraudulence. An insolvency regulation such as the one in Finland (which is good at striking a balance between protecting and restructuring inherently healthy firms, discouraging rent seeking, and still encouraging entrepreneurial risk taking) is only feasible when countries also rank highly on the rule of law, government effectiveness and the security of property rights.

Certainly, this is no easy undertaking. Portugal and Slovenia provide what may be seen as a second-best solution in this respect. Given their apparent success, it is probably a wise, low-risk strategy for countries with similar institutional configurations to undertake reforms akin to theirs, so as not to base their reform strategy on high-quality legal institutions that are in fact absent.

3.7   R&D, Commercialization and Knowledge Spillovers

3.7.1   Preamble

The successful exploitation of research and inventions combined with the transfer and spillover of the related knowledge stimulates growth and prosperity in a modern economy (e.g., Acs et al. 2009 and Baumol 2010). Entrepreneurs play an important role in this respect in both new and established ventures, by virtue of their ability to recognize unexploited opportunities in the market and to spread innovations by imitation and incremental improvements of existing technologies (Baumol 2002). An important objective of entrepreneurship policy must be to promote this process of production and commercialization of knowledge.

In the early phase of industrialization in the West, leading innovators were mostly people with little formal education whose innovations emanated from practical experience in workshops and production plants. This gradually changed when specialized engineering schools were formed in the late 19th century both in Europe and the United States, followed by the formation of R&D departments in the large engineering firms (Rosenberg and Birdzell 1986, Chap. 8; Mowery and Rosenberg 1998). However, even today, the common idea that more R&D spending is the tool that will promote innovation reveals an overly mechanical view of how the entrepreneurial ecosystem works. New knowledge and inventions are only the first step in an innovation and commercialization process. For increased R&D to translate into economic growth, entrepreneurs must exploit the inventions by introducing new methods of production or new products in the marketplace (Bhidé 2008; Michelacci 2003).

Neither Bill Gates nor Henry Ford invented the technologies used in their ventures, but in their role as entrepreneurs, they were needed to successfully exploit inventions that someone else had created. The EOE perspective illustrates this forcefully through its emphasis on the need for a number of different actors and competencies to fully realize the benefits of innovation. Limiting the focus to inventions and R&D misses the bulk of the story, and although high R&D spending can be a necessary component of a successful economy, it is far from sufficient. Increased R&D will not automatically bring forth entrepreneurs—perhaps it is even the other way around; in an economic system that rewards productive entrepreneurship, a great deal of R&D is undertaken because the results flowing from R&D are *demanded* (Holcombe 2007).

The knowledge spillover theory of entrepreneurship offers a complimentary view (Acs et al. 2009; Braunerhjelm et al. 2010), which is important for several reasons. First, and in the vein of Schumpeter (1934), it distinguishes between knowledge in general and *economic* knowledge (i.e., knowledge that is economically exploitable) and conjectures that more knowledge (more R&D) does not automatically translate into more economic knowledge. Second, this theory rejects the assumption that (economic) knowledge automatically spills over and induces growth. Rather, the theory highlights the importance of the entrepreneur in enabling these crucial transformations. The entrepreneur is the actor who transforms knowledge into economic knowledge through the commercialization of inventions, and the one who brings about knowledge spillovers throughout the economy.

Knowledge is often tacit, sticky and uncertain, making it costly and difficult to transmit and evaluate (Arrow 1962). As the innovative process is shrouded in uncertainty, the expected value and variance of an innovation will differ across individuals—a discrepancy that creates high profit opportunities for entrepreneurial firms or spinoffs in instances when incumbent firms do not recognize or realize a profit opportunity.

Furthermore, innovation and entrepreneurship are largely localized phenomena, and innovation capabilities originate from the interplay between generic knowledge and learning processes that are embedded in regional knowledge and market environments (Zucker et al. 1998). A critical mass seems to be required for a dynamic innovation environment to emerge since there are many benefits for firms located close to other firms in dense, knowledge-intensive areas (Feldman 1994; Feldman and Audretsch 1999; Paci and Usai 1999; Ejermo 2009; Delgado et al. 2014).

Such dense environments are characterized by distinct wage and productivity premiums—strong centripetal forces that attract both individuals and firms (Puga 2010). Glaeser and Mare (2001), for example, report a wage premium in the U.S. of 33% between the largest metropolitan areas and non-urban locations. Such effects are also reported for European countries (Di Addario and Patacchini 2008; Andersson et al. 2014; D'Costa and Overman 2014). The evidence also suggests that the existence of strong clusters in a region enhances growth opportunities in other industries and clusters (Delgado et al. 2014).

3.7.2 Reform Agenda

Table 3.7 reveals that expenditure on R&D currently constitutes a sizable share of GDP in rich countries. In the EU, the total R&D spending ranges from roughly 3% of GDP in the Nordic countries, Germany and Austria (slightly higher than the U.S. level) to below 1% in most Eastern European and Mediterranean countries (column 1). Importantly, among top spenders, as much as 70% of total R&D spending is made by firms; the rest is spent by the government, primarily through the funding of academic research (columns 2 and 3). Furthermore, the business sector share of R&D is substantially lower in countries that have a low overall spending on R&D with the government share normally exceeding 50%. The ranking of countries is thus highly similar when comparing R&D spending by business enterprises.

The variation across Europe is further accentuated when considering that the number of researchers engaged in R&D per million inhabitants is almost ten times higher in Denmark at the top compared to Cyprus at the bottom (column 4). Nevertheless, as argued above, R&D spending and the number of researchers per capita are input measures. Output from the R&D sector is economically valuable

Table 3.7 Total gross expenditure on R&D and business R&D spending (BERD) as a share of GDP (2014), number of researchers per million population (2014), number of patent families relative to GDP (2012), and direct and indirect (tax incentives) government support of business R&D (2013)

Country	Total gross R&D expenditure	Business R&D spending (BERD)	Gov't share of R&D spending	No. of researchers per million	Patent families	Gov't funding, % of total BERD
Finland	3.17	2.15	0.32	6,986	8.38	3.3
Sweden	3.16	2.12	0.33	6,868	7.74	6.6
Denmark	3.08	1.98	0.36	7,198	4.27	6.1
Austria	3.00[b]	2.11[b]	0.30	4,815	4.28	12.8
Germany	2.84	1.93	0.32	4,460	5.87	4.0
USA	2.73[a]	1.92[a]	0.30	4,019[c]	2.75	13.5[c]
Belgium	2.46	1.76	0.70	4,176	2.12	17.0[c]
Slovenia	2.39	1.85	0.23	4,145	1.69	18.4
France	2.26	1.46	0.35	4,201	3.52	25.3
Czech Rep.	2.00	1.12	0.44	3,418	0.68	16.1
Netherlands	1.97	1.11	0.44	4,478	3.43	15.3
UK	1.70	1.10	0.35	4,252	2.22	14.5
Ireland	1.52	1.11	0.27	3,732	1.69	20.7[c]
Estonia	1.43	0.62	0.57	3,271	0.47	12.9
Hungary	1.37	0.98	0.28	2,651	0.55	32.7
Italy	1.29	0.72	0.57	2,007	1.68	6.9
Portugal	1.29	0.59	0.54	3,700	0.39	22.0
Luxembourg	1.26	0.66	0.60	4,577	6.24	
Spain	1.22	0.64	0.48	2,641	0.69	15.6[c]
Lithuania	1.01	0.30	0.70	2,962	0.37	
Poland	0.94	0.44	0.50	2,037	0.48	9.1
Slovakia	0.89	0.33	0.63	2,718	0.30	6.1
Malta	0.85	0.51	0.40	2,133	2.48	
Greece	0.83	0.28	0.66	2,699	0.35	21.4
Croatia	0.79	0.38	0.52	1,437	0.20	
Bulgaria	0.78	0.51	0.35	1,818	0.29	
Latvia	0.69	0.25	0.64	1,884	0.27	
Cyprus	0.47	0.08	0.83	750	0.73	
Romania	0.38	0.16	0.58	922	0.11	

Note [a]2013; [b]2015; [c]2012
Source R&D expenditure: UNESCO Institute for Statistics, UIS online database (2007–15). Researchers: UNESCO Institute for Statistics, UIS online database (2007–14). Patents: World Intellectual Property Organization, WIPO Statistics Database; International Monetary Fund, World Economic Outlook Database, October 2015 (PPP$ GDP) (2007–12). Government support: *OECD Science, Technology and Industry Scoreboard 2015*

knowledge and innovations. One such measure consists of the number of patents per capita (column 5). Indeed, we can see a strong cross-country correlation between R&D spending and the rate of patenting.[26]

Increased R&D spending can thus be associated with an increased production of economically valuable knowledge, as measured by the rate of patenting. However, this does not imply that a policy of increased government R&D spending will automatically result in more economically valuable knowledge. First, patents are not the only way of measuring new economic knowledge; when Da Rin et al. (2006) examined 14 European countries in a panel between 1988 and 2001, they did not find any positive relationship between public R&D spending and the rate of innovation, which they defined as the share of high-tech and early-stage venture capital investments. Furthermore, as shown in the last column of Table 3.7, the share of R&D in the business sector that is directly or indirectly funded by the government is lowest in countries with the highest R&D spending by business enterprises (see Appendix Table A.2 for a more detailed overview).

In line with our previous discussion, this suggests that higher spending on R&D does not automatically produce more innovations or more entrepreneurial activity. Instead, if a well-functioning entrepreneurial ecosystem is not already in place, the full potential from increased R&D cannot be reaped. Therefore, quantitative R&D goals risk becoming a waste of resources, as focus and resources are directed towards factors that would have found a better use elsewhere in the economy. Instead, in an economic system encouraging productive entrepreneurship, a great deal of R&D is undertaken because the results from R&D are *demanded*. Here, entrepreneurs and demanding customers in the ecology's skill structure serve as particularly crucial sources of information regarding consumer needs and preferences (von Hippel et al. 2011).

Policymakers cannot hope to offset deficiencies in other policy areas by directly favoring R&D. In line with the argument in Sect. 2.2, the main role of the government should be to enable and facilitate rather than to subsidize certain industries or firms. Most importantly, governments should adhere to the late Steven Klepper's (2016) persuasive findings that strong and highly dynamic industry clusters could emerge anywhere and gain momentum through entrepreneurial spinoffs from the leading firms. The implication is clear: it should be easy to start a business, and incentives for individuals to behave entrepreneurially and grow the new businesses should be strong. However, it is still important to avoid spoiling the strong tradition in many European countries of harboring innovations, even of a radical kind, inside large firms through intrapreneurship (Stam and Stenkula 2017).

Research also reveals that geographic proximity facilitates knowledge spillover and knowledge transfer, suggesting a potential role for the government in promoting networks, clusters and urbanization. Appendix Table A.3 shows the prevalence of clusters in European economies and the United States, revealing that clusters are

---

[26]Of course, the number of patents is not a perfect measure of innovation either (Boldrin and Levine 2013).

considerably more common in Western European countries than in Eastern European and Mediterranean countries. If cluster policy enables more transfer of knowledge between businesses and organizations, entrepreneurship may be facilitated as a result (Moretti 2012; Moretti and Thulin 2013). For example, well-functioning housing markets, where the prices reflect scarcity and preferences, are necessary conditions for continued growth in dense areas (Glaeser 2008, 2011), as is an adequate infrastructure that allows for smooth transportation and commuting.

However, this form of support should not be directed to specific firms; instead, firms must self-select and not be "picked". Policymakers would do well to remember that cluster formation is a long-term process that cannot be accelerated by means of a quick policy fix. By contrast, when different policies complement and reinforce one another, region-specific connections and institutions evolve and adapt over time in a complex interaction that often becomes a key component of a region's competitive advantage (Gertler 2004; Wolfe and Gertler 2006).

3.8 Incentives for Human Capital Investment

3.8.1 Preamble

Economic growth and prosperity depend to a large extent on human capital—economically valuable knowledge tied to and inseparable from the individual (see, e.g., Barro 2001). Human capital can be acquired in many ways, such as through formal schooling, formal and informal on-the-job training, labor market programs and retraining, and informal experience and the cultivation of personal interest. There is little doubt that the incentives to invest in human capital are important for growth, a view strongly supported by the economic growth literature (Lucas 1988; Mankiw et al. 1992).

In particular, human capital of a mathematical and natural science orientation is deemed to be important for science-based entrepreneurship (Shavinina 2013). Successful entrepreneurial ventures are often highly dependent on academically trained and motivated individuals. People who engage in knowledge-based entrepreneurship can have many different backgrounds, such as university faculties, other firms, and the general pool of individuals with a graduate or an undergraduate degree.

According to human capital theory (Schultz 1960; Becker 1964), the decision to acquire and use human capital can be analyzed as an individual investment decision governed by the rate of return on human capital, often measured as the relative increase in the individual's (discounted lifetime increase in) wage that can be attributed to an additional year of schooling. However, such an educational premium before tax is an imperfect measure of the true rate of return on education, which is also determined by factors such as the progressivity of the tax system, the availability of scholarships and subsidized loans,[27] tuition fees, the age at the time of graduation, and the continually changing risk of becoming unemployed.

Hence, government policy can influence the incentives and opportunities for individuals to acquire human capital in numerous ways. The most obvious measure is by directly allocating public funds to the educational system. Even more potent is the way policy incentivizes agents in the educational system itself, and how such activities and policies can complement or act as a substitute for the training provided by employers. In addition, as discussed in the previous sections, income taxes, wage differentials, and a well-designed social insurance system are important components in making it beneficial to acquire productive knowledge that is subsequently used intensively. Overall, it may be said that this incentivization requires substantial knowledge of the strategic choices individuals make over the course of their many years of human capital formation.

The first strategic choice occurs in high school when the individual decides whether to enter the labor market or to proceed to a university. If the individual enrolls in a university, he or she faces a choice between science- and technology-based disciplines (or STEM fields—science, technology, engineering, and math) and other areas. At graduation, the natural science graduates can again choose between employment and graduate studies with the objective of obtaining a Ph.D., but the quality of the educational system at the primary and secondary levels largely determines how much can be demanded from students at the tertiary level. If the quality of their previous education has been deficient, fewer students will be willing or able to choose more analytically demanding lines of study. Finally, after receiving a Ph.D., the individual faces yet another choice between a university career and other employment.

Obviously, all links must function efficiently for knowledge-based entrepreneurship to flourish. There must be sufficient incentives (i) to invest in human capital at the university level, (ii) to become involved in knowledge-based entrepreneurial ventures, and (iii) to adjust the university subject areas to bring them into line with business sector demand and to facilitate the transfer of knowledge from academia to the entrepreneurial sector. This third factor can be expected to have complex repercussions for the individual's decisions at every stage. The incentives in the university system will directly influence the propensity of faculty members to become involved in entrepreneurial ventures while also affecting the educational choices of students.

---

[27]The effect of subsidized loans and scholarships on human capital investment is particularly difficult to assess. It is trivially true that, *ceteris paribus*, the rate of return for attending a university increases (Edin and Holmlund 1995). However, loan subsidies and scholarships boost the rate of return by giving rise to income during studies as opposed to educational premiums that give rise to (higher) income after completion of the studies. Thus, loan subsidies and scholarships that are not correlated with the rate of return for the training are likely to lower the incentives to choose the type of education that provides the most human capital investment as measured by the rate of return in terms of relative wages. This effect is reinforced if there is no tuition.

If the rate of return on schooling is low, individuals can partly adjust by basing their educational choice more on what they enjoy to study than on what might be beneficial to them in their subsequent careers, seeing education more as a consumption good and less as an investment in human capital. This might include a lower willingness to opt for demanding lines of study that deprive students of leisure time or prevent them from working part-time. Hence, human capital investment may be endogenous in the sense that individuals adjust their actual investment in human capital (as opposed to the number of years of schooling) to the institutionally given rate of return.

Empirical research reveals a positive correlation between formal education and informal human capital investment in the form of on-the-job training (Mincer 1984; Heckman 2000). At the same time, strong incentives for such training may partially substitute for weak incentives for formal education, and the wage structure may also encourage intense and efficient use of the individual's human capital.

In this respect, it is important to note that successful entrepreneurs in the United States tend to have advanced degrees.[28] Strong educational credentials are also common among European billionaire entrepreneurs. This is likely due to the causal effect of human capital and access to new ideas and to the fact that unusually talented individuals are selected into elite universities. Potential entrepreneurs face several educational and career choices, especially early in life. If the incentives to seek advanced education are distorted, individuals could make choices that make them less likely to acquire the type of knowledge that is valuable to entrepreneurial firms.

Moreover, entrepreneurial firms must be able to recruit highly competent people. The entrepreneurial sector in Silicon Valley has evolved in close cooperation with academic research at adjacent Stanford University. Europe's lack of elite universities (outside of the United Kingdom) compared to the United States is likely to be a disadvantage for the European Union's ability to develop Schumpeterian entrepreneurship.[29]

In contrast to the university systems in most European countries, the American university system is decentralized and intensely competitive. American universities retain a high degree of autonomy; thus, they can pursue opportunities to solve their own problems and to build on their own unique strengths and aspirations. Competition occurs along several dimensions: (i) competition among universities for students and among professors for the best students at the graduate level;

---

[28]Many so-called super-entrepreneurs, i.e., entrepreneurs who built billion dollar fortunes by starting and growing their own companies, have acquired extensive human capital. In the U.S., one third of super-entrepreneurs have a degree from an elite university such as Harvard, Stanford or the University of Chicago, compared to less than 1% of the total labor force (Henrekson and Sanandaji 2014).

[29]Except for UK universities, only six of the 50 highest ranked universities in the world come from EU member countries according to *The Times Higher Education World University Rankings* 2015–2016 (https://www.timeshighereducation.com/world-university-rankings/2016/world-ranking#!/page/0/length/25/sort_by/rank/sort_order/asc/cols/stats).

(ii) competition among universities for the best professors in a cultural and economic context in which mobility is high; and (iii) competition among professors for research support, giving them time away from teaching and access to complementary resources. That said, the European university systems do have some advantages relative to the U.S. system, especially because they have no or low tuition fees, which makes the best universities affordable regardless of one's social background. The challenge for Europe is to retain its openness while increasing the quality of its universities.

3.8.2 Reform Agenda

The first column of Table 3.8 reveals surprisingly large differences in educational expenditures as a share of GDP across EU countries, where spending can differ by as much as a factor of three. The three Nordic countries are at the top, while the bottom is dominated by Eastern European countries and Italy. Yet high spending is not everything. The important thing to ask is, first, to what extent does high spending translate into more knowledge among students? Secondly, to what extent is this knowledge economic, i.e., useful in production?

Arguably, the best source available for answering these questions comes from OECD's Programme for International Student Assessment (PISA). The most comprehensive study to date finds a strong and statistically robust relationship between national economic performance and the level of knowledge as measured in internationally comparable tests, such as PISA and TIMSS (Hanushek and Woessman (2015).[30] PISA test results in mathematics, science and reading for the year 2012 are presented in columns 2–4 in Table 3.8.

Table 3.8 makes clear that high educational spending can be associated with top results (Finland) as well as weak results (Sweden). Conversely, pupils in Poland and Estonia have excellent results despite relatively low educational spending, while Romania and Bulgaria spend little and do poorly. (In all three areas, Chinese pupils are outstanding.) In the United States, allegedly the most innovative and entrepreneurial of all countries, government spending on education is intermediate, but complementary private spending is substantial (2% of GDP compared to an EU average of 0.3% of GDP; see OECD 2015b, p. 207). Thus, despite high total spending, U.S. pupils perform below average in all three areas and poorly in mathematics.

---

[30]The PISA survey was created by the OECD as a response to member countries' demand for a reliable metric of pupils' knowledge and skills. Every three years, nationally representative samples of 15-year old pupils take a test in mathematical, reading and scientific literacy. The number of participants has increased over time; in the 2012 survey, 65 countries and economies were represented (OECD 2013). TIMSS stands for Trends in International Mathematics and Science Study and is a test given every four years since 1995 in mathematics and science to 11- and 15-year-olds (Mullis et al. 2012a, b).

Table 3.8 Expenditure on education as a share of GDP in EU countries and the U.S., 2012, and PISA results (in reading, mathematics, and science) in EU countries and the U.S., 2012

Country	Education spending	Country	PISA mathematics	Country	PISA science	Country	PISA reading
Denmark (2011)	8.55	Netherlands	523	Finland	545	Finland	524
Sweden	7.66	Estonia	521	Estonia	541	Ireland	523
Finland	7.19	Finland	519	Poland	526	Poland	518
Malta	6.76	Poland	518	Germany	524	Estonia	516
Cyprus (2011)	6.64	Belgium	515	Ireland	522	Netherlands	511
Belgium (2011)	6.37	Germany	514	Netherlands	522	Belgium	509
Ireland	5.84	Austria	506	UK	514	Germany	508
UK (2013)	5.72	Ireland	501	Slovenia	514	France	505
Slovenia	5.66	Slovenia	501	Czech Rep.	508	UK	499
France	5.53	Denmark	500	Austria	506	USA	498
Netherlands	5.51	Czech Rep.	499	Belgium	505	Denmark	496
Austria	5.45	France	495	Latvia	502	Czech Rep.	493
USA (2011)	5.22	UK	494	France	499	Austria	490
Portugal (2011)	5.12	Latvia	491	Denmark	498	Italy	490
Germany	4.95	Luxembourg	490	USA	497	Latvia	489
Poland (2011)	4.86	Portugal	487	Spain	496	Spain	488
Estonia	4.79	Italy	485	Lithuania	496	Hungary	488
Lithuania	4.79	Spain	484	Italy	494	Luxembourg	488
Hungary	4.65	Slovakia	482	Hungary	494	Portugal	488
Spain	4.37	USA	481	Luxembourg	491	Croatia	485
Czech Rep.	4.26	Lithuania	479	Croatia	491	Sweden	483
Croatia (2011)	4.16	Sweden	478	Portugal	489	Slovenia	481
Italy (2011)	4.14	Hungary	477	Sweden	485	Lithuania	477

(continued)

Table 3.8 (continued)

Country	Education spending	Country	PISA mathematics	Country	PISA science	Country	PISA reading
Slovakia	3.94	Croatia	471	Slovakia	471	Greece	477
Bulgaria	3.59	Greece	453	Greece	467	Slovakia	463
Latvia	3.20	Romania	445	Bulgaria	446	Cyprus	449
Romania	2.99	Cyprus	440	Romania	439	Romania	438
		Bulgaria	439	Cyprus	438	Bulgaria	436

Note Malta did not participate in the PISA test. The scores are calculated in each year so that the mean is 500 and the standard deviation 100

Source OECD Programme for International Student Assessment (PISA)

Hence, it appears that even though educational expenditure can be potentially beneficial for the generation of economic knowledge, there is a great risk that the money is spent inefficiently. However, poorly performing countries clearly have plenty of room to learn how to organize "production" in the education sector more efficiently.

In this respect, it is notable that tertiary enrollment has exploded in recent decades, which is evident from the first column of Table 3.9. The enrolment rate is very high in many of the poorest EU countries, notably Greece, Bulgaria and the Baltic countries. However, high enrolment rates per se are no guarantee that university studies have a high social rate of return. The resources per student vary enormously across fields, countries and schools (van der Ploeg and Veugelers 2008), but the humanities and social sciences are generally far less costly than the STEM fields, and there is an obvious temptation for policymakers to expand inexpensive programs in order to boost university enrolment, since this is a relatively inexpensive way of giving the impression of investing a lot in human capital. Such actions would be illusory, and the damage would be exacerbated if such measures crowd out existing non-academic post-secondary education and vocational training at the upper secondary level. Traditionally, such education has been important in central European countries (see Appendix Fig. A.3).

A high enrolment rate may also conceal the fact that many of those who enroll never manage to complete their studies, which, as mentioned, depends on whether previous education levels have equipped them with the ability and willingness to do so. In Slovenia and Sweden, a mere 47 and 53%, respectively, have completed their Bachelor's program three years after scheduled graduation. The corresponding figures in the United Kingdom and the United States are 84 and 78%, respectively (see the rightmost column of Table 3.10). A deficient quality at lower levels of education may also cause fewer students to choose more analytically demanding disciplines (see the second column of Table 3.9).

As mentioned, the decision to acquire and use economically valuable human capital is ultimately an individual investment decision governed to a considerable extent by the rate of return on human capital (Schultz 1960; Becker 1964). Table 3.10 presents two arguably imperfect measures of this rate of return. The first column demonstrates that the rate of return on schooling varies greatly across countries from the United States, Germany and Poland at the top to Denmark, Italy and Sweden at the bottom. Comparing the overall rate of return with the return on analytical/numerical ability in the second column underscores the vital importance of this type of knowledge.

These findings merit an additional discussion, notably related to the differences in the university systems in Europe compared to the United States, the features of which were briefly discussed in Sect. 3.8.1. The U.S. university system seems more responsive to the economic needs of society than the university systems in most European countries. High tuition fees mean that students expect a high degree of relevance from the offered curricula. Likewise, professors who are dependent on research grants are more likely to adjust their research to fields that have high economic value (Rosenberg 2000). Decentralization and competition in the

Table 3.9 Tertiary enrolment and graduates in science and engineering in EU countries and the U.S., 2013

Country	Tertiary enrolment (%)	Graduates in S & E (%)
Greece	110.2	28.7[a]
Finland	91.1	27.9
USA	88.8	14.9
Spain	87.1	22.2[a]
Slovenia	85.2	24.7[a]
Denmark	81.2	20.4
Austria	80.0[b]	27.9
Netherlands	78.5[a]	14.4[a]
Ireland	73.2	23.8[a]
Estonia	72.9	22.1[a]
Belgium	72.3	16.4[a]
Lithuania	72.0	22.2
Poland	71.2	17.4
Bulgaria	70.8[b]	20.1
Latvia	67.0	17.9
Portugal	66.2	26.1
Czech Rep.	65.4	23.2
Italy	63.5	20.2[a]
Sweden	63.4	25.7
France	62.2	24.5
Croatia	61.7[a]	23.9[a]
Germany	61.1	
Hungary	57.0	16.8[a]
UK	56.9	25.2
Slovakia	54.4	20.5
Cyprus	53.1[b]	19.0
Romania	52.2	25.5
Malta	45.1[b]	19.1[a]
Luxembourg	19.4[a]	16.3

Note [a]2012; [b]2014. The ratio of total tertiary enrolment, regardless of age, to the population of the age group that officially corresponds to the tertiary level of education. Tertiary education, whether or not aiming at an advanced research qualification, normally requires, as a minimum condition of admission, the successful completion of education at the secondary level. Graduates in science and engineering is defined as the share of all tertiary graduates in science, manufacturing, engineering, and construction over all tertiary graduates (n/a Germany)
Source UNESCO Institute for Statistics, UIS online database (2007–14)

American system also result in greater wage dispersion with salaries being more likely to reflect the economic relevance of a field and the professor's achievements in research and teaching. Entirely new fields and major breakthroughs in established fields have been rapidly introduced to the curricula of leading U.S. universities over the years.

Table 3.10 Before tax educational premiums and completion rates in EU countries and the U.S.

Country	Educational premium	Country	Return on analytical/numerical ability	Completion rate, %
USA	11.1	USA	27.9	78
Poland	10.1	Ireland	24.1	94
Germany	9.5	Germany	23.5	n/a
Slovakia	9.5	Spain	22.8	n/a
Cyprus	8.9	UK	22.5	84
UK	8.5	Poland	19.1	n/a
Ireland	8.5	Netherlands	18.3	66
Netherlands	8.2	Austria	17.9	78
Spain	7.9	Slovakia	17.9	n/a
Austria	7.7	Estonia	17.9	51
Estonia	7.4	France	17.4	70
Finland	6.8	Belgium	14.9	n/a
Belgium	6.2	Finland	14.2	n/a
Czech Rep.	5.9	Cyprus	13.8	n/a
France	5.5	Denmark	13.7	81
Denmark	5.5	Italy	13.2	n/a
Italy	5.3	Czech Rep.	12.4	60
Sweden	4.2	Sweden	12.1	53

Note The educational premium is defined as the relative increase in the wage that can be attributed to an additional year of schooling. The return on analytical/numerical ability is defined as the relative increase in the wage that results from a one standard deviation increase in a person's PIAAC score for numeracy. All EU countries in the Hanushek et al. study are included in the table. The completion rate is defined as the share of student's who entered a Bachelor's Program that have graduated six years later (2014)
Source Hanushek et al. (2015) and OECD (2016, p. 175)

The challenge for Europe is to remain accessible to everyone regardless of social background while increasing the quality of its universities to establish more world-class universities in the EU (outside of the United Kingdom). To meet this challenge, it must first be recognized that most European university systems are highly centralized; universities tend to be government owned, and the entry of private universities is disallowed or highly restricted (Jongbloed 2010). The government typically grants charters to universities and determines the rules of admission and the university's size (through budgetary allocations) as well as the size of specific fields of study. Such control makes individual institutions less flexible, for example when it comes to varying remuneration based on an individual professor's research and teaching performances or according to the economic value of the professor's field. A high degree of centralization also makes it more difficult for individual universities to adjust the allocation of research budgets across fields in response to changing demands outside of academia.

While it would be unrealistic to believe that European countries could mimic the U.S. university system, certain steps could be taken to level the playing field. Notably, the link between universities and external stakeholders could be strengthened (see Appendix Table A.4). Google and Netscape provide two interesting examples of innovations originating from university campuses (in both cases from a private university). Learning from such examples would facilitate the stimulation of academic entrepreneurship and accelerate the commercialization of university-developed innovations of great potential value (Goldfarb and Henrekson 2003; Kauffman Foundation 2007). For this to be successful, university faculty must encourage and stimulate entrepreneurial initiatives while incentives for university spinoffs remain strong. Some universities have a Technology Transfer Office (TTO), an in-house organization specializing in assisting academic entrepreneurs in commercializing their inventions. However, a TTO could also hinder the commercialization of useful technologies by making the process too bureaucratic and focusing on its own narrowly defined proprietary interests and key performance indicators (Baumol et al. 2007; Kauffman Foundation 2008). Given the U.S. evidence, we are hesitant to advocate this route.

In the Horizon 2020 initiative, the EU states:

> By coupling research and innovation, Horizon 2020 is helping to achieve this with its emphasis on excellent science, industrial leadership and tackling societal challenges. The goal is to ensure Europe produces world-class science, removes barriers to innovation and makes it easier for the public and private sectors to work together in delivering innovation.[31]

If the EU is serious about achieving this goal, universities and other public institutions of learning need to become more entrepreneurial, flexible and adaptive towards market demand. Again, the challenge is to find the right balance between quality and accessibility and to be sensitive to the more egalitarian educational tradition in Europe while making the system of higher learning more dynamic and responsive to the needs of the entrepreneurial ecosystem.

3.9 Informal Institutions

3.9.1 Preamble

Informal institutions are typically described as the customs, traditions, and norms that permeate society (Williamson 1998, 2000), and they are arguably of great relevance to entrepreneurship and innovation. This is partly because informal institutions affect the workings of formal institutions; they can function as substitutes for formal institutions in reducing transaction costs (Arrow 1972; Glaeser et al. 2002), and the law derives much of its value from the respect that it enjoys by

---

[31]https://ec.europa.eu/programmes/horizon2020/en/what-horizon-2020.

being consistent with these informal institutions (Kasper et al. 2012; cf. Becker and Murphy 2000). The flipside of the coin is that reforms of formal institutions may prove counterproductive if undertaking them destroys the existing benefits of informal institutions (Berkowitz et al. 2003; Lundström and Stevenson 2005; Dixit 2009; Ebner 2009).

Informal institutions are also important to entrepreneurship in their own right. McCloskey (2016) argues that the norms regarding honorable and appropriate behavior have been important historically for entrepreneurship and economic development; when people promote and honor entrepreneurs and their virtues, the floodgates of economic development will open (cf. Goldstone 1987; Mokyr 1992). Other cultural factors, such as individualism, power distance, uncertainty avoidance, masculinity and self-expressive values, have also been revealed as drivers of innovation and entrepreneurship (Shane 2003; Hechavarria and Reynolds 2009; Taylor and Wilson 2012).

Furthermore, trust, already identified as a generally important determinant for enabling economic coordination, efficiency and growth (Knack and Keefer 1997; Zak and Knack 2001; Karlan 2005; Sabatini 2008; Pugno and Verme 2012), has become a variable of increasing interest for entrepreneurship scholars (Welter and Smallbone 2006; Welter 2012). High-trust environments are said to foster market entry, enterprise growth and productive entrepreneurship (Fukuyama 1996; cf. Welter and Smallbone 2006), and individual trust is believed to be of fundamental importance for supporting network relations (Jack et al. 2004; Kim and Aldrich 2005; Anderson et al. 2007). As a lubricant without which network activity could not be possible (Anderson and Jack 2002), trust is therefore immediately relevant for a better functioning entrepreneurial ecosystem of the kind envisioned in Chap. 2 with the potential to affect all nodes in the skill structure.

In summary, informal institutions affect the workings of formal institutions, but they are also important for the fostering of entrepreneurship in their own right. The social legitimacy of entrepreneurs is especially important in this respect.

3.9.2 Reform Agenda

Above, we identified trust as a fundamental informal institution for economic efficiency as well as entrepreneurship. In fact, it might arguably take precedence over other cultural factors, such as attitudes towards entrepreneurship, competition or individualism.[32] The point can perhaps best be illustrated by plotting the EU countries with respect to their level of trust and their attitude towards competition, which is done in Fig. 3.8.

---

[32]As shown in Stam and Stenkula (2017), trust may be an important explanation for the high level of intrapreneurship in Sweden and the other Nordic countries.

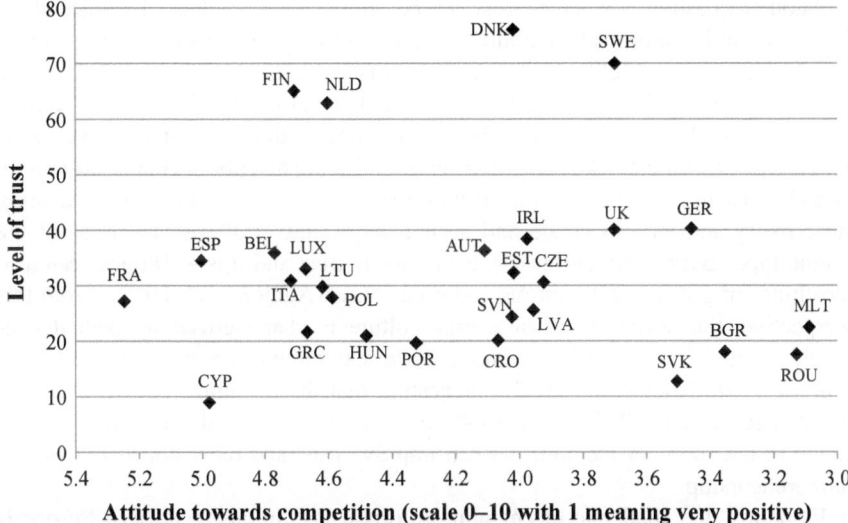

Fig. 3.8 Trust and attitudes toward competition in EU countries. *Note* The figure is based on V62 (share of people who claim that most people can be trusted), and V196 (mean on a scale from 1–10 with 1 meaning "Competition is good. It stimulates people to work hard and develop new ideas", and 10 meaning "Competition is harmful. It brings out the worst in people.") *Source* European Value Survey 2008

In terms of views towards competition, countries from Eastern Europe and the Mediterranean are among those that view it most favorably (Malta, Bulgaria, Romania and Slovakia) *and* least favorably (Spain and Cyprus). This suggests that the attitude towards competition is a poor determinant of innovation and entrepreneurship in and of itself. Meanwhile, whereas the Mediterranean countries and parts of Eastern Europe score low on trust, the Nordic countries and the Netherlands score exceptionally high. Of these high-trust countries, Sweden stands out as having the most positive attitude towards competition. High-trust countries are also more individualistic and less worried about uncertainty. With a generally high-trusting pattern, Western European countries exhibit high degrees of individualism *and* are better at dealing with (or worry less about) uncertainty, whereas Eastern European and Mediterranean countries exhibit more collectivism and worry more about uncertainty. These patterns can be seen in Figs. A.4–A.6 in the Appendix.

One way of interpreting these correlations is that promoting competition in a low-trust environment is likely to prove futile or even detrimental. Though it may lead to entrepreneurship, it is likely to be of an unproductive or even destructive nature (cf. Baumol 1990). By contrast, a more positive view of competition is likely to be beneficial for productive entrepreneurship in a high-trust environment.

Another question is whether trust can be promoted. A number of studies claim that trust can be improved by political means. Notably, the positive cross-country correlation between welfare-state size and trust is taken as evidence that certain types of welfare policies can produce trust and social capital (Barr 2004; Kumlin and Rothstein 2005; Uslaner and Rothstein 2005) or that more free market institutions can increase trust levels (Berggren and Jordahl 2006). Others argue that overall, causality should be reversed with historically high-trust populations being more likely and able to create and sustain large, universal welfare states of the Nordic type (Bergh and Bjørnskov 2011), while trust and trustworthiness can also substitute for government controls and regulations (Aghion et al. 2010). From this perspective, the development of a trust culture is characterized by path dependencies and spirals fueled by unique historical circumstances (Humphrey and Schmitz 1998; Nooteboom 2002), suggesting that the evolution of a trust culture can take generations (Williamson 2000). In sum, this suggests that it is unlikely that policy in the short- or medium-run can improve trust and other norms relevant to entrepreneurship.

Evidently, the challenge of changing informal institutions in Eastern Europe is the most urgent but also the most difficult. The informal institutions in these countries evolved in the Soviet-dominated system, which made low trust a necessity for the people. With the fall of the Eastern bloc, a rapid shift occurred towards a capitalist system, the functioning of which would have benefitted greatly from higher trust and a greater tolerance towards uncertainty. These cultural changes have yet to materialize. Hence, while increased trust levels would evidently improve the conditions for innovation and entrepreneurship, policy is unlikely to be able to induce that change.

3.10 Summary and Conclusions: Institutions Nurturing a More Entrepreneurial Europe

The discussion in the previous sections of this chapter is summarized in Table 3.11, assigning to each policy area the general prescription regarding the characteristics required for a regime fostering entrepreneurship and innovation.

Table 3.11 Institutions and policy measures that support an entrepreneurial economy

Policy area	Characteristics
Rule of law and the protection of property rights	
– General	Stable and secure
– Intellectual property rights	Balance interests of inventors against need for knowledge diffusion
Taxation	
– Earned income tax rate	Low or moderate
– Capital income tax rate	Low
– Capital gains tax rate	Low
– Tax on stock options	Low
– Degree of tax neutrality across owner categories	High
– Degree of tax neutrality across sources of finance	High
– Personal taxation on asset holdings	Zero, or exemption for equity holdings
– Corporate tax rate	Low or moderate statutory rate, effective rate equal to statutory rate and neutral across types of firms and industries
Savings, capital and finance	
– Wealth formation	Support private wealth formation
– Venture capital	Indirect support
Labor markets	
– Labor security mandates	Portable tenure rights
Social security	
– Design	Portable entitlements
– Unemployment insurance	Flexicurity

(continued)

Table 3.11 (continued)

Policy area	Characteristics
Regulatory entry and growth barriers	
– Entry barriers	Low
– International trade	Openness
– Production of welfare services/merit goods	Sizeable private production, contestability
– Financing of welfare services/merit goods	Government ensures basic high-quality supply, then private financing
– Profit-driven organizations	Fully allowed within the framework of well-designed regulations
Bankruptcy law and insolvency regulation	Relatively generous and allow for a "second chance"
R&D, commercialization and knowledge spillover	No quantitative goals, no targeted support, indirect support, enabling and general
Incentives for human capital investment	Good incentives to acquire valuable knowledge and skills through formal education and at work; incentives to supply such opportunities by the educational system itself
Informal institutions	Norms and habits that facilitate cooperation and impersonal exchange, notably trust

References

Acemoglu, D., & Johnson, S. (2005). Unbundling institutions. *Journal of Political Economy, 113* (5), 947–997.

Acemoglu, D., Johnson, S., & Robinson, J. A. (2001). The colonial origins of comparative development: An empirical investigation. *American Economic Review, 91*(5), 1369–1401.

Acs, Z. J., Audretsch, D. B., Braunerhjelm, P., & Carlsson, B. (2009). The knowledge spillover theory of entrepreneurship. *Small Business Economics, 32*(1), 15–30.

Acs, Z. J., & Sanders, M. (2012). Patents, knowledge spillovers, and entrepreneurship. *Small Business Economics, 39*(4), 801–817.

Acs, Z. J., & Szerb, L. (2007). Entrepreneurship, economic growth and public policy. *Small Business Economics, 28*(2–3), 109–122.

Aghion, P., Algan, Y., Cahuc, P., & Shleifer, A. (2010). Regulations and distrust. *Quarterly Journal of Economics, 125*(3), 1015–1049.

Alstadsæter, A., Jacob, M., & Michaely, R. (2014). *Do dividend taxes affect corporate investment?* CESifo Working Paper No. 4931. Munich: CESifo Group.

Andersen, T. M. (2005). The Danish labor market—From excess to shortage. In M. Werding (Ed.), *Structural unemployment in Western Europe: Reasons and remedies.* Cambridge, MA: MIT Press.

Anderson, A. R., & Jack, S. L. (2002). The articulation of social capital in entrepreneurial networks: A glue or a lubricant? *Entrepreneurship & Regional Development, 14*(3), 193–210.

Anderson, A. R., Park, J., & Jack, S. L. (2007). Entrepreneurial social capital. *International Small Business Journal, 25*(3), 245–272.

Andersson, F., & Jordahl, H. (2013). Outsourcing public services: Ownership, competition, quality and contracting. IFN Working Paper No. 874. Stockholm: Research Institute of Industrial Economics.

Andersson, M., Klaesson, J., & Larsson, J. P. (2014). The sources of the urban wage premium by worker skills: Spatial sorting or agglomeration economies? *Papers in Regional Science, 93*(4), 727–747.

Armour, J., & Cumming, D. (2008). Bankruptcy law and entrepreneurship. *American Law and Economics Review, 10*(2), 303–350.

Arrow, K. J. (1962). Economic welfare and the allocation of resources for invention. In R. R. Nelson (Ed.), *The rate and direction of inventive activity: Economic and social factors* (pp. 609–626). Princeton, NJ: Princeton University Press.

Arrow, K. J. (1972). Gifts and exchanges. *Philosophy & Public Affairs, 1*(4), 343–362.

Audretsch, D. B., Carree, M. A., van Stel, A. J., & Thurik, A. R. (2002). Impeded industrial restructuring: The growth penalty. *Kyklos, 55*(1), 81–97.

Audretsch, D. B., & Thurik, A. R. (2000). Capitalism and democracy in the 21st century: From the managed to the entrepreneurial economy. *Journal of Evolutionary Economics, 10*(1), 17–34.

Autio, E., Kronlund, M., & Kovalainen, A. (2007). *High-growth SME support initiatives in nine countries: Analysis, categorization, and recommendations.* Helsinki: Ministry of Trade and Industry.

Bandiera, O. (2003). Land reform, the market for protection, and the origins of the Sicilian Mafia: Theory and evidence. *Journal of Law Economics and Organization, 19*(1), 218–244.

Barr, N. (2004). *The economics of the welfare state.* Oxford: Oxford University Press.

Barro, R. J. (2001). Human capital and growth. *American Economic Review, 91*(2), 12–17.

Battilana, J., Leca, B., & Boxenbaum, E. (2009). How actors change institutions: Towards a theory of institutional entrepreneurship. *Academy of Management Annals, 3*(1), 65–107.

Baumol, W. J. (1990). Entrepreneurship: Productive, unproductive, and destructive. *Journal of Political Economy, 98*(5), 893–921.

Baumol, W. J. (2002). *The free-market innovation machine: Analyzing the growth miracle of capitalism.* Princeton, NJ: Princeton University Press.

Baumol, W. J. (2010). *The microtheory of innovative entrepreneurship*. Princeton, NJ: Princeton University Press.

Baumol, W. J., Litan, R. E., & Schramm, C. J. (2007). *Good capitalism, bad capitalism and the economics of growth and prosperity*. New Haven, CT and London: Yale University Press.

Béchard, J.-P., & Grégoire, D. (2005). Entrepreneurship education research revisited: The case of higher education. *Academy of Management Learning and Education, 4*(1), 22–43.

Becker, B., & Josephson, J. (2016). Insolvency resolution and the missing high-yield bond markets. *Review of Financial Studies, 29*(10), 814–849.

Becker, G. S. (1964). *Human capital: A theoretical and empirical analysis, with special reference to education*. Chicago, IL: University of Chicago Press.

Becker, G. S., & Murphy, K. M. (2000). *Social economics: Market behavior in a social environment*. Boston, MA: Harvard University Press.

Begley, T. M., Tan, W.-L., & Schoch, H. (2005). Politico-economic factors associated with interest in starting a business: A multi-country study. *Entrepreneurship Theory and Practice, 29*(1), 35–55.

Bengtsson, O., & Hand, J. (2013). Employee compensation in entrepreneurial companies. *Journal of Economics and Management Strategy, 22*(2), 312–340.

Berggren, N., & Jordahl, H. (2006). Free to trust? Economic freedom and social capital. *Kyklos,* 141–169.

Bergh, A., & Bjørnskov, C. (2011). Historical trust levels predict the current size of the welfare state. *Kyklos, 64*(1), 1–19.

Bergman, M., Johansson, P., Lundberg, S., & Spagnolo, G. (2016). Privatization and quality: Evidence from elderly care in Sweden. *Journal of Health Economics, 49*(September), 109–119.

Berkowitz, D., Pistor, K., & Richard, J.-F. (2003). Economic development, legality, and the transplant effect. *European Economic Review, 47*(1), 165–195.

Besley, T., & Ghatak, M. (2010). Property rights and economic development. In D. Rodrik & M. R. Rosenzweig (Eds.), *Handbook of development economics* (Vol. 5, pp. 4525–4595). Amsterdam: North-Holland.

Bhidé, A. (2008). *The venturesome economy: How innovation sustains prosperity in a more connected world*. Princeton, NJ: Princeton University Press.

Birch, D. (2006). What have we learned? *Foundations and Trends in Entrepreneurship, 2*(3), 57–62.

Boldrin, M., & Levine, D. K. (2013). The case against patents. *Journal of Economic Perspectives, 27*(1), 3–22.

Bottazzi, L., & Da Rin, M. (2002). Venture capital in Europe and the financing of innovative companies. *Economic Policy, 17*(34), 229–270.

Boyns, N., Cox, M., Spires, R., & Hughes, A. (2003). *Research into the enterprise investment scheme and venture capital trusts*. Wellington, NZ: PACEC Report for Inland Revenue.

Braguinsky, S., Branstetter, L. G., & Regateiro, A. (2011). The incredible shrinking Portuguese firm. NBER Working Paper No. 17265. Cambridge, MA: National Bureau of Economic Research.

Braunerhjelm, P., Acs, Z. J., Audretsch, D. B., & Carlsson, B. (2010). The missing link: Knowledge diffusion and entrepreneurship in endogenous growth. *Small Business Economics, 34*(2), 105–125.

Bygrave, W. D., & Hunt, S. A. (2004). *Global entrepreneurship monitor (GEM) 2004 financing report*. Wellesley and London: Babson College and London Business School.

Caballero, R. J., & Hammour, M. L. (2000). Creative destruction and development: Institutions, crises and restructuring. NBER Working Paper No. 7849. Cambridge, MA: National Bureau of Economic Research.

Carroll, R., Holtz-Eakin, D., Rider, M., & Rosen, H. S. (2000). Income taxes and entrepreneurs' use of labor. *Journal of Labor Economics, 18*(2), 324–355.

Chetty, R., Friedman, J., Olsen, T., & Pistaferri, L. (2011). Adjustment costs, firm responses, and micro vs. macro labor supply elasticities: Evidence from Danish tax records. *Quarterly Journal of Economics, 126*(2), 749–804.

Chetty, R., Looney, A., & Kroft, K. (2009). Salience and taxation: theory and evidence. *American Economic Review, 99*(4), 1145–1177.

Chetty, R., & Saez, E. (2005). Dividend taxes and corporate behavior: Evidence from the 2003 dividend tax cut. *Quarterly Journal of Economics, 120*(3), 791–833.

Cohen, W. M. (2005). Patents and appropriation: Concerns and evidence. *Journal of Technology Transfer, 30*(1–2), 57–71.

Cullen, J. B., & Gordon, R. H. (2007). Taxes and entrepreneurial risk-taking: Theory and evidence in the U.S. *Journal of Public Economics, 91*(7–8), 1479–1505.

Cumming, D. (2005). Agency costs, institutions, learning, and taxation in venture capital contracting. *Journal of Business Venturing, 20*(5), 573–622.

Cumming, D. (2012). Venture capital financial contracting: An overview of the international evidence. In H. Landström & C. Mason (Eds.), *Handbook of research on venture capital* (Vol. 2). Cheltenham, UK and Northampton, MA: Edward Elgar.

D'Costa, S., & Overman, H. G. (2014). The urban wage growth premium: Sorting or learning? *Regional Science and Urban Economics, 48*(September), 168–179.

Da Rin, M., Nicodano, G., & Sembenelli, A. (2006). Public policy and the creation of active venture capital markets. *Journal of Public Economics, 90*(8–9), 1699–1723.

Dana, L. P. (1990). Saint Martin/Sint Maarten: A case study of the effects of culture on economic development. *Journal of Small Business Management, 28*(4), 91–98.

Davis, S. J., & Henrekson, M. (1999). Explaining national differences in the size and industry distribution of employment. *Small Business Economics, 12*(1), 59–83.

De Soto, H. (2000). *The mystery of capital: Why capitalism triumphs in the west and fails everywhere else.* New York, NY: Basic Books.

Delgado, M., Porter, M. E., & Stern, S. (2014). Clusters, convergence, and economic performance. *Research Policy, 43*(10), 1785–1799.

Delmar, F., Wennberg, K., Wiklund, J., & Sjöberg, K. (2005). *Self-employment among the Swedish science and technology labor force: The evolution of firms between 1990 and 2000.* Report A2005:001. Östersund: Swedish Institute for Growth Policy Studies.

Desai, M., Gompers, P., & Lerner, J. (2003). Institutions, capital constraints and entrepreneurial firm dynamics: Evidence from Europe. NBER Working Paper No. 10165. Cambridge, MA: National Bureau of Economic Research.

Di Addario, S., & Patacchini, E. (2008). Wages and the city. Evidence from Italy. *Labour Economics, 15*(5), 1040–1061.

Dixit, A. K. (2009). Governance, institutions and economic activity. *American Economic Review, 99*(1), 3–24.

Djankov, S., Glaeser, E., La Porta, R., Lopez-de-Silanes, F., & Shleifer, A. (2003). The new comparative economics. *Journal of Comparative Economics, 31*(4), 595–619.

Djankov, S., & Murrell, P. (2002). Enterprise restructuring in transition: A quantitative survey. *Journal of Economic Literature, 40*(3), 739–792.

Domar, E. D., & Musgrave, R. A. (1944). Proportional income taxation and risk sharing. *Quarterly Journal of Economics, 48*(3), 388–422.

Douhan, R., & Henrekson, M. (2010). Entrepreneurship and second-best institutions: Going beyond Baumol's typology. *Journal of Evolutionary Economics, 20*(4), 629–643.

Ebbinghaus, B. (Ed.). (2011). *The varieties of pension governance: Pension privatization in Europe.* Oxford: Oxford University Press.

Eberhart, R. N., Eesley, C. E., & Eisenhardt, K. M. (2017). Failure is an option: Institutional change, entrepreneurial risk, and new firm growth. *Organization Science, 28*(1), 93–112.

Ebner, A. (2009). Entrepreneurial state: The Schumpeterian theory of industrial policy and the East Asian 'miracle'. In U. Cantner, J.-L. Gaffard, & L. Nesta (Eds.), *Schumpeterian perspectives on innovation, competition, and growth.* Berlin: Springer.

Edin, P.-A., & Holmlund, B. (1995). The Swedish wage structure: The rise and fall of solidarity wage policy? In R. B. Freeman & L. F. Katz (Eds.), *Differences and changes in wage structures.* Chicago, IL: University of Chicago Press.

Ejermo, O. (2009). Regional innovation measured by patent data—Does quality matter? *Industry and Innovation, 16*(2), 141–165.

Elert, N., & Henrekson, M. (2017). Status quo institutions and the benefits of institutional deviations. *International Review of Entrepreneurship, 15*(1), forthcoming.

Emons, W. (1997). Credence goods and fraudulent experts. *Rand Journal of Economics, 28*(1), 107–120.

Erixon, F., & Weigel, B. (2016). *The innovation illusion: How so little is created by so many working so hard.* New Haven, CT: Yale University Press.

European Commission (2008). *Think small first. A small business act for Europe.* DG Enterprise. Brussels: European Commission.

European Commission (2015). *Upgrading the single market: More opportunities for business and people.* Communication from the Commission to the European Parliament, The Council, The European Economic and Social Committee and the Committee of the Regions. https://ec.europa.eu/transparency/regdoc/rep/1/2015/EN/1-2015-550-EN-F1-1.PDF. Accessed December 6, 2016.

Feldman, M. P. (1994). *The geography of innovations.* Dordrecht, NL and Boston, MI: Kluwer Academic Publishers.

Feldman, M. P., & Audretsch, D. B. (1999). Innovation in cities: Science-based diversity, specialization and localized monopoly. *European Economic Review, 43*(2), 409–429.

Fenn, G., Liang, N., & Prowse, S. (1995). *The economics of the private equity market.* Washington, D.C.: Board of Governors of the Federal Reserve System.

Fogel, R. W. (1999). Catching up with the economy. *American Economic Review, 89*(1), 1–21.

Francis, F. (1996). *Trust: The social virtues and the creation of prosperity.* New York: Free Press/Penguin Books.

Gans, J. S., & Persson, L. (2013). Entrepreneurial commercialization choices and the interaction between IPR and competition policy. *Industrial and Corporate Change, 22*(1), 131–151.

Garicano, L., Lelarge, C., & Van Reenen, J. (2016). Firm size distortions and the productivity distribution: Evidence from France. *American Economic Review, 106*(11), 3439–3479.

Gentry, W. M., & Hubbard, R. G. (2000). Tax policy and entrepreneurial entry. *American Economic Review, 90*(2), 283–287.

Gertler, M. S. (2004). *Manufacturing culture: The institutional geography of industrial practice.* Oxford: Oxford University Press.

Gilbert, B. A., Audretsch, D. B., & McDougall, P. P. (2004). The emergence of entrepreneurship policy. *Small Business Economics, 22*(3–4), 313–323.

Gilson, R. J., & Schizer, D. M. (2003). Understanding venture capital structure: A tax explanation for convertible preferred stock. *Harvard Law Review, 116*(3), 874–916.

Glaeser, E. L. (2008). The rise of the sunbelt. *Southern Economic Journal, 74*(3), 610–643.

Glaeser, E. L. (2011). *Triumph of the city: How our greatest invention makes us richer, smarter, greener, healthier, and happier.* New York: Penguin Press.

Glaeser, E. L., Laibson, D., & Sacerdote, B. (2002). An economic approach to social capital. *Economic Journal, 112*(483), F437–F458.

Glaeser, E. L., & Mare, D. C. (2001). Cities and skills. *Journal of Labor Economics, 19*(2), 316–342.

Gnyawali, D. R., & Fogel, D. S. (1994). Environments for entrepreneurship development: Key dimensions and research implications. *Entrepreneurship Theory and Practice, 18*(4), 43–62.

Goldfarb, B., & Henrekson, M. (2003). Bottom-up versus top-down policies towards the commercialization of university intellectual property. *Research Policy, 32*(4), 639–658.

Goldstone, J. A. (1987). Cultural orthodoxy, risk, and innovation: The divergence of east and west in the early modern world. *Sociological Theory, 5*(2), 119–135.

Gompers, P. A., & Lerner, J. (1999). An analysis of compensation in the U.S. venture capital partnership. *Journal of Financial Economics, 51*(1), 3–44.

Gompers, P. A., & Lerner, J. (2001). *The money of invention: How venture capital creates new wealth.* Cambridge, MA: Harvard Business School Press.

Gompers, P. A., & Lerner, J. (2004). *The venture capital cycle* (2nd ed.). Cambridge, MA: MIT Press.

Gompers, P. A., Lerner, J., & Kovner, A. (2009). Specialization and success: Evidence from venture capital. *Journal of Economics and Management Strategy, 18*(3), 817–844.

Grant Thornton (2016). *Konkurrenskraften i svensk ägarbeskattning.* Stockholm: Confederation of Swedish Enterprise.

Gruber, J., & Saez, E. (2002). The elasticity of taxable income: Evidence and implications. *Journal of Public Economics, 84*(1), 1–32.

Gwartney, J., Lawson, R., & Hall, J. (2015). *Economic freedom of the world: 2015 annual report.* Vancouver, BC: Fraser Institute.

Hanushek, E. A., Schwert, G., Widerhold, S., & Woessmann, L. (2015). Returns to skills around the world: Evidence from PIAAC. *European Economic Review, 73*(January), 103–130.

Hanushek, E. A., & Woessmann, L. (2015). *The knowledge capital of nations: Education and the economics of growth.* Cambridge, MA: MIT Press.

Harju, J., & Kosonen, T. (2013). *The impact of tax incentives on the economic activity of entrepreneurs.* Government Institute for Economic Research Working Paper No. 42, Helsinki.

Hechavarria, D. M., & Reynolds, P. D. (2009). Cultural norms & business start-ups: The impact of national values on opportunity and necessity entrepreneurs. *International Entrepreneurship and Management Journal, 5*(4), 417–437.

Heckman, J. J., & Lochner, L. (2000). Rethinking myths about education and training: Understanding the sources of skill formation in a modern economy. In S. Danzinger & J. Waldfogel (Eds.), *Securing the future: Investing in children from birth to college.* New York: Russell Sage Foundation.

Heim, B. T. (2010). The responsiveness of self-employment income to tax rate changes. *Labour Economics, 17*(6), 940–950.

Henrekson, M., & Rosenberg, N. (2001). Designing efficient institutions for science-based entrepreneurship: Lessons from the U.S. and Sweden. *Journal of Technology Transfer, 26*(2), 207–231.

Henrekson, M., & Sanandaji, T. (2014). Small business activity does not measure entrepreneurship. *Proceedings of the National Academy of Sciences (PNAS), 111*(5), 1760–1765.

Henrekson, M., & Sanandaji, T. (2016a). Stock option taxation and venture capital activity: A cross-country comparison. IFN Working Paper No 1104. Stockholm: Research Institute of Industrial Economics.

Henrekson, M., & Sanandaji, T. (2016b). Owner-level taxes and business activity. *Foundations and Trends in Entrepreneurship, 12*(1), 1–101.

Ho, Y.-P., & Wong, P.-K. (2007). Financing, regulatory costs and entrepreneurial propensity. *Small Business Economics, 28*(2–3), 187–204.

Hofer, H. (2007). *The severance pay reform in Austria ("Abfertigung Neu").* CESifo DICE Report 4/2007, 41–48.

Holbrook, D., Cohen, W. M., Hounshell, D. A., & Klepper, S. (2000). The nature, sources, and consequences of firm differences in the early history of the semiconductor industry. *Strategic Management Journal, 21*(10–11), 1017–1041.

Holcombe, R. G. (2007). *Entrepreneurship and economic progress.* New York: Routledge.

Huizinga, H., Laeven, L., & Nicodeme, G. (2008). Capital structure and international debt shifting. *Journal of Financial Economics, 88*(1), 80–118.

Humphrey, J., & Schmitz, H. (1998). Trust and inter-firm relations in developing and transition economies. *Journal of Development Studies, 34*(4), 32–61.

Hurst, E., & Lusardi, A. (2004). Liquidity constraints, household wealth, and entrepreneurship. *Journal of Political Economy, 112*(2), 319–347.

Ilmakunnas, P., & Kanniainen, V. (2001). Entrepreneurship, economic risks, and risk insurance in the welfare state: Results with OECD data 1978–93. *German Economic Review, 2*(3), 195–218.

Invest Europe (2016). *2015 European private equity activity statistics on fundraising, investments & divestments*. Brussels: Invest Europe.

Jack, S. L., Dodd, S. D., & Anderson, A. R. (2004). Social structures and entrepreneurial networks: The strength of strong ties. *International Journal of Entrepreneurship and Innovation, 5*(2), 107–120.

Jaffe, A. B., & Lerner, J. (2004). *Invention and its discontents: How our broken patent system is endangering innovation and progress, and what to do about it*. Princeton, NJ: Princeton University Press.

Johnson, S., McMillan, J., & Woodruff, C. (2002). Property rights and finance. *American Economic Review, 92*(5), 1335–1356.

Jongbloed, B. (2010). *Funding higher education: A view across Europe*. Report within the MODERN Project, European Platform for Higher Education Modernisation. Twente, NL: Center for Higher Education Policy Studies, University of Twente.

Kaplan, S., & Lerner, J. (2010). It ain't broke: The past, present, and future of venture capital. *Journal of Applied Corporate Finance, 22*(2), 36–47.

Karlan, D. S. (2005). Using experimental economics to measure social capital and predict financial decisions. *American Economic Review, 95*(5), 1688–1699.

Kasper, W., Streit, M. E., & Boettke, P. J. (2012). *Institutional economics: Property, competition, policies*. Cheltenham, UK and Northampton, MA: Edward Elgar.

Kauffman Foundation (2007). On the road to an entrepreneurial economy: A research and policy guide. Ewing Marion Kauffman Foundation Working Paper, July.

Kauffman Foundation (2008). Entrepreneurship summit: Executive summary. Ewing Marion Kauffman Foundation and the International Economic Development Council Working Paper, September.

Kay, J. (2004). *The truth about markets*. London: Penguin.

Keuschnigg, C., & Nielsen, S. B. (2004a). Taxation and venture capital backed entrepreneurship. *International Tax and Public Finance, 11*(4), 369–390.

Keuschnigg, C., & Nielsen, S. B. (2004b). Start-ups, venture capitalists, and the capital gains tax. *Journal of Public Economics, 88*(5), 1011–1042.

Kim, P. H., & Aldrich, H. E. (2005). *Social capital and entrepreneurship*. Hanover, MA: Now Publishers.

Kleiner, M. M. (2006). *Licensing occupations: Ensuring quality or restricting competition?* Kalamazoo, MI: W.E. Upjohn Institute.

Klepper, S. (2016). *Experimental capitalism: The nanoeconomics of American high-tech industries*. Princeton, NJ: Princeton University Press.

Kleven, H. J., & Schultz, E. (2014). Estimating taxable income responses using Danish tax reforms. *American Economic Journal: Economic Policy, 6*(4), 271–301.

Knack, S., & Keefer, P. (1997). Does social capital have an economic payoff? A cross-country investigation. *Quarterly Journal of Economics, 112*(4), 1251–1288.

Koellinger, P., & Minniti, M. (2009). Unemployment benefits crowd out entrepreneurial activity. *Economics Letters, 103*(2), 96–98.

Kumlin, S., & Rothstein, B. (2005). Making and breaking social capital: The impact of welfare-state institutions. *Comparative Political Studies, 38*(4), 339–365.

Kuratko, D. (2005). The emergence of entrepreneurship education: Development, trends, and challenges. *Entrepreneurship Theory and Practice, 29*(5), 577–597.

La Porta, R., Lopes-de-Silanes, F., Schleifer, A., & Vishny, R. (1997). Trust in large organizations. *American Economic Review, 87*(2), 333–338.

Lawton, T., McGuire, S., & Rajwani, T. (2013). Corporate political activity: A literature review and research agenda. *International Journal of Management Reviews, 15*(1), 86–105.

Le Grand, J., & Bartlett, W. (1993). The theory of quasi markets. In J. Le Grand & W. Bartlett (Eds.), *Quasi markets and social policy*. London: Palgrave Macmillan.

Lerner, J. (2009). *Boulevard of broken dreams: Why public efforts to boost entrepreneurship and venture capital have failed—And what to do about it*. Princeton, NJ: Princeton University Press.

Lerner, J., & Tåg, J. (2013). Institutions and venture capital. *Industrial and Corporate Change, 22* (1), 153–182.

Levine, R. (2005). Finance and growth: Theory and evidence. In P. Aghion & S. Durlauf (Eds.), *Handbook of economic growth* (Vol. 1A). Amsterdam: North-Holland.

Libecap, G. D. (1993). *Contracting for property rights.* New York: Cambridge University Press.

Liebregts, W. J. (2016). Institutional explanations for patterns of entrepreneurial activity: The case of the Dutch task market. FIRES Deliverable D5.3.

Lindbeck, A. (1982). Tax effects versus budget effects on labor supply. *Economic Inquiry, 20*(3), 473–489.

Lucas, R. E. (1988). On the mechanics of economic development. *Journal of Monetary Economics, 22*(1), 3–42.

Lundström, A., & Stevenson, L. A. (2005). *Entrepreneurship policy: Theory and practice.* New York, NY: Springer.

Mankiw, N. G., Romer, D., & Weil, D. N. (1992). A contribution to the empirics of economic growth. *Quarterly Journal of Economics, 107*(2), 407–437.

Martin, J., & Scarpetta, S. (2012). Setting it right: Employment protection, labour reallocation and productivity. *De Economist, 160*(2), 89–116.

Mason, C. M. (2006). Informal sources of venture finance. In S. C. Parker (Ed.), *The life cycle of entrepreneurial ventures.* International Handbook on Entrepreneurship Series (Vol. 3). New York: Springer.

McCloskey, D. N. (2016). *Bourgeois equality: How ideas, not capital or institutions, enriched the world.* Chicago, IL: University of Chicago Press.

Merrill, S. A., Levin, R. C., & Myers, M. B. (2004). *A patent system for the 21st century.* Washington, D.C.: National Academic Press.

Michelacci, C. (2003). Low returns to R&D due to the lack of entrepreneurial skills. *Economic Journal, 113*(484), 207–225.

Milhaupt, C. J., & West, M. D. (2000). The dark side of private ordering: An institutional and empirical analysis of organized crime. *University of Chicago Law Review, 67*(1), 41–98.

Mincer, J. (1984). Human capital and economic growth. *Economics of Education Review, 3*(3), 195–205.

Misher, N. (1984). Tax consequences of exercising an incentive stock option with stock of the granting corporation. *The Tax Executive,* 357–363.

Mokyr, J. (1992). *The lever of riches: Technological creativity and economic progress.* Oxford: Oxford Paperbacks.

Moretti, E. (2012). *The new geography of jobs.* New York, NY: Houghton Mifflin Harcourt.

Moretti, E., & Thulin, P. (2013). Local multipliers and human capital in the United States and Sweden. *Industrial and Corporate Change, 22*(1), 131–151.

Mowery, D., & Rosenberg, N. (1998). *Paths of innovation: Technological change in 20th century America.* Cambridge and New York, NY: Cambridge University Press.

Mullis, I. V. S., Martin, M. O., Foy, P., & Arora, A. (2012a). *TIMSS 2011 international results in mathematics.* Chestnut Hill, MA: TIMSS & PIRLS International Study Center, Boston College.

Mullis, I. V. S., Martin, M. O., Foy, P., & Arora, A. (2012b). *TIMSS 2011 international results in science.* Chestnut Hill, MA: TIMSS & PIRLS International Study Center, Boston College.

Nickell, S. J. (1997). Unemployment and labor market rigidities: Europe versus North America. *Journal of Economic Perspectives, 11*(3), 55–74.

Niehof, J. (1999). *Barriers for hiring personnel.* Research Report 9807/E. Zoetermeer: EIM Business and Policy Research.

Nikos, M., Chittenden, F., & Poutziouris, P. (1999). Financial policy and capital structure choice in UK SMEs: Empirical evidence from company panel data. *Small Business Economics, 12*(2), 113–130.

Nooteboom, B. (2002). *Trust: Forms, foundations, functions, failures and figures.* Cheltenham, UK and Northampton, MA: Edward Elgar.

Nooteboom, B. (2014). *How markets work and fail, and what to make of them*. Cheltenham, UK and Northampton, MA: Edward Elgar.

Norbäck, P.-J., & Persson, L. (2009). The organization of the innovation industry: Entrepreneurs, venture capitalists, and oligopolists. *Journal of the European Economic Association, 7*(6), 1261–1290.

Norbäck, P.-J., & Persson, L. (2012). Entrepreneurial innovations, competition and competition policy. *European Economic Review, 56*(3), 488–506.

North, D. C., & Weingast, B. R. (1989). Constitutions and commitment: The evolution of institutions governing public choice in seventeenth-century England. *Journal of Economic History, 49*(4), 803–832.

Nykvist, J. (2008). Entrepreneurship and liquidity constraints: Evidence from Sweden. *Scandinavian Journal of Economics, 110*(1), 23–43.

OECD (1998) *Fostering entrepreneurship*. Paris: OECD.

OECD (2000). *OECD employment outlook*. Paris: OECD.

OECD (2003). *The sources of economic growth in the OECD countries*. Paris: OECD.

OECD (2005). *Small and medium enterprise and entrepreneurship outlook*. Paris: OECD.

OECD (2007). *OECD framework for the evaluation of SME and entrepreneurship policies and programmes*. Paris: OECD.

OECD (2013). *PISA 2012 results: What students know and can do: Student performance in mathematics, reading and science* (Vol. 1). Paris: OECD Publishing.

OECD (2015a). *Taxation of SMEs in OECD and G20 countries*. Paris: OECD.

OECD (2015b). *Pension funds in figures*. Paris: OECD. Available online: https://www.oecd.org/finance/Pension-funds-pre-data-2015.pdf. Accessed October 16, 2016.

OECD (2016). *OECD employment outlook 2016*. Paris: OECD.

Paci, R., & Usai, S. (1999). Externalities, knowledge spillovers and the spatial distribution of innovation. *GeoJournal, 49*(4), 381–390.

Parker, S. C. (2009). *The economics of entrepreneurship*. Cambridge: Cambridge University Press.

Pelikan, P. (1988). Can the imperfect innovation systems of capitalism be outperformed? In G. Dosi et al. (Eds.), *Technical change and economic theory*. London: Pinter Publishers.

Poschke, M. (2013). Who becomes an entrepreneur? Labor Market prospects and occupational choice. *Journal of Economic Dynamics and Control, 37*(3), 693–710.

Puga, D. (2010). The magnitude and causes of agglomeration economies. *Journal of Regional Science, 50*(1), 203–219.

Pugno, M., & Verme, P. (2012). *Life satisfaction, social capital and the bonding-bridging nexus*. World Bank Working Paper No. 5945. Washington, D.C.: World Bank.

Puri, M., & Zarutskie, R. (2012). On the life cycle dynamics of venture-capital- and non-venture-capital-financed firms. *Journal of Finance, 67*(6), 2247–2293.

Riksbanken (2014). Det kollektiva pensionssparandets betydelse i det svenska finansiella systemet. *Ekonomiska Kommentarer 3/2014*. Stockholm: The Riksbank, Sweden's central bank.

Rodrik, D. (2007). *One economics, many recipes: Globalization, institutions, and economic growth*. Princeton, NJ and Oxford: Princeton University Press.

Rodrik, D. (2008). Second-best institutions. *American Economic Review, 98*(2), 100–104.

Rodrik, D., Subramanian, A., & Trebbi, F. (2004). Institutions rule: The primacy of institutions over geography and integration in economic development. *Journal of Economic Growth, 9*(2), 131–165.

Rosen, S. (1983). Specialization and human capital. *Journal of Labor Economics, 1*(1), 43–49.

Rosen, H. S. (2005). Entrepreneurship and taxation: Empirical evidence. In V. Kanniainen & C. Keuschnigg (Eds.), *Venture capital, entrepreneurship, and public policy* (pp. 251–279). Cambridge, MA: MIT Press.

Rosenberg, N. (2000). American universities as endogenous institutions. In *Schumpeter and the endogeneity of technology: Some American perspectives*. London: Routledge.

Rosenberg, N., & Birdzell, L. E. (1986). *How the west grew rich: The economic transformation of the industrial world*. New York: Basic Books.

Rydqvist, K., Spizman, J., & Strebulaev, I. (2014). Government policy and ownership of equity securities. *Journal of Financial Economics, 111*(1), 70–85.

Sabatini, F. (2008). Social capital and the quality of economic development. *Kyklos, 61*(3), 466–499.

Saez, E., Slemrod, J., & Giertz, S. H. (2012). The elasticity of taxable income with respect to marginal tax rates: A critical review. *Journal of Economic Literature, 50*(1), 3–50.

Scarpetta, S., Hemmings, P., Tressel, T., & Woo, J. (2002). *The role of policy and institutions for productivity and firm dynamics: Evidence from micro and industry data.* OECD Economics Department Working Paper No. 329. Paris: OECD Publishing.

Schäfer, W., Kroneman, M., Boerma, W., van den Berg, M., Westert, G., Devillé, W., et al. (2010). The Netherlands: Health system review. *Health Systems in Transition, 12*(1). Copenhagen: European Observatory on Health Systems and Policies.

Schivardi, F., & Torrini, R. (2008). Identifying the effects of firing restrictions through size-contingent differences in regulation. *Labour Economics, 15*(3), 482–511.

Schultz, T. W. (1960). Capital formation by education. *Journal of Political Economy, 68*(6), 571–583.

Schumpeter, J. A. (1934). *The theory of economic development: An inquiry into profits, capital, credit, interest and the business cycle.* Cambridge, MA: Harvard University Press.

Shane, S. A. (2003). *A general theory of entrepreneurship: The individual-opportunity nexus.* Cheltenham, UK and Northampton, MA: Edward Elgar.

Shane, S. A. (2008). *The illusions of entrepreneurship.* New Haven, CT and London: Yale University Press.

Shavinina, L. V. (Ed.) (2013). *The Routledge international handbook of innovation education.* New York, NY: Routledge.

Siegel, D. S., Wessner, C., Binks, M., & Lockett, A. (2003). Policies promoting innovation in small firms: Evidence from the U.S. and U.K. *Small Business Economics, 20*(2), 121–127.

Sinn, H. W. (1996). Social insurance, incentives and risk taking. *International Tax and Public Finance, 3*(3), 259–280.

Skedinger, P. (2010). *Employment protection legislation. Evolution, effects, winners and losers.* Cheltenham, UK, and Northampton, MA: Edward Elgar.

Sørensen, P. B. (2010). *Swedish tax policy: Recent trends and future challenges.* Report to the Expert Group on Public Economics 2010:4. Stockholm: Ministry of Finance.

Stam, E., & Stenkula, M. (2017). Intrapreneurship in Sweden: An international perspective. FIRES Working Paper No. 17−02.

Stigler, G. J. (1971). The theory of economic regulation. *Bell Journal of Economics and Management Science, 2*(1), 3–21.

Svensk Försäkring (2015). *Svensk Försäkring i siffror 2015: Preliminära uppgifter för verksamhetsåret 2015.* Stockholm: Insurance Sweden.

Svensson, R. (2008). Growth through research and development—What does the research literature say? In *Vinnova Report VR 2008:19.* Stockholm: Vinnova.

Taylor, M. Z., & Wilson, S. (2012). Does culture still matter? The effects of individualism on national innovation rates. *Journal of Business Venturing, 27*(2), 234–247.

Ucbasaran, D., Alsos, G. A., Westhead, P., & Wright, M. (2008). Habitual entrepreneurs. *Foundations and Trends in Entrepreneurship, 4*(4), 309–450.

Uslaner, E. M., & Rothstein, B. (2005). All for one: Equality, corruption, and social trust. *World Politics, 58*(1), 41–72.

van Auken, H. E. (1999). Obstacles to business start-up. *Journal of Developmental Entrepreneurship, 4*(Fall/Winter), 175–187.

van der Ploeg, F., & Veugelers, R. (2008). Higher education reform and the renewed Lisbon Strategy: Role of member states and the European Commission. In G. Gelauff, I. Grilo, & A. Lejour (Eds.), *Subsidiarity and economic reform in Europe.* Berlin and Heidelberg: Springer.

van Stel, A., Storey, D., & Thurik, A. R. (2007). The effect of business regulations on nascent and young business entrepreneurship. *Small Business Economics, 28*(2–3), 171–186.

von Hippel, E., Ogawa, S., & de Jong, J. P. J. (2011). The age of the consumer-innovator. *MIT Sloan Management Review, 53*(1), 27–35.

Wagner, R. E. (2014). Entangled political economy: A keynote address. In S. Horwitz & R. Koppl (Eds.), *Entangled political economy*. Advances in Austrian Economics (Vol. 18). London: Emerald.

Welter, F., & Smallbone, D. (2006). Exploring the role of trust in entrepreneurial activity. *Entrepreneurship Theory and Practice, 30*(4), 465–475.

Welter, F. (2012). All you need is trust? A critical review of the trust and entrepreneurship literature. *International Small Business Journal, 30*(3), 193–212.

Williamson, O. E. (1998). Transaction cost economics: How it works; where it is headed. *De Economist, 146*(1), 23–58.

Williamson, O. E. (2000). The new institutional economics: Taking stock, looking ahead. *Journal of Economic Literature, 38*(3), 595–613.

Wolfe, D. A., & Gertler, M. S. (2006). Local antecedents and trigger events: Policy implications of path dependence for cluster formation. In P. Braunerhjelm & M. P. Feldman (Eds.), *Cluster genesis: Technology-based industrial development*. Oxford: Oxford University Press.

Zak, P. J., & Knack, S. (2001). Trust and growth. *Economic Journal, 111*(470), 295–321.

Zucker, L. G., Darby, M. R., & Brewer, M. B. (1998). Intellectual human capital and the birth of U.S. biotechnology enterprises. *American Economic Review, 88*(1), 290–306.

Chapter 4
Summary and Conclusions

Abstract To promote innovation and economic growth in the European Union, we propose a reform strategy with respect to the aforementioned nine areas, which we consider to be the most pertinent institutions and policies in order to foster a productive entrepreneurial economy. Overall, the proposed institutional changes move in a liberalizing direction, but we acknowledge that one-size-fits-all policy reforms aimed at freer markets will not necessarily be successful. Instead, a successful reform strategy must consider country differences that affect the viability of reform. Nevertheless, policymakers should not lose sight of the long-term goal of institutional liberalization to promote entrepreneurship, innovation and growth. Hopefully, this work inspires both confidence and humility regarding Europe's innovation future.

Keywords Entrepreneurship · European Union · Innovation · Institutions · Policy reform · Regulation · Self-employment

The purpose of this study has been to propose an institutional reform strategy to enhance innovation and entrepreneurial activity in Europe. In doing so, we acknowledged the existence of several types of capitalism among the EU member countries. These types have evolved into highly complex entities that are held together by a number of complementary institutions. None of these models consistently exhibits superior performance in terms of social welfare, making it difficult to determine which model the European Union as a whole should strive to converge towards.

The observation that the European Union overall suffers from a lack of innovation motivates the analysis in this study. We identify entrepreneurship and innovation as the relevant aspects that policy reforms should strive to improve. Entrepreneurship and innovation are crucial for the growth of the polities in which they occur and for their effect on growth on a global scale. An innovation is the translation of an idea or an invention into an economically valuable good or service, and if it can cross borders the innovation can be implemented to the benefit of the inhabitants of countries far different from the one in which it originated.

N. Elert et al., *Institutional Reform for Innovation and Entrepreneurship*,
SpringerBriefs in Economics, DOI 10.1007/978-3-319-55092-3_4

It is increasingly understood that innovation is important for the European Union and its member states, as evidenced by the broad consensus on the political goal that the Union become more innovative and entrepreneurial. The most appropriate strategy to achieve this goal is a complicated issue. Should all member countries adopt reform packages that make them more alike, further increasing the political and economic convergence that has been ushered in by years of negotiation and collaboration? Or should those member states that can reasonably be classified as belonging to the same variety of capitalism espouse a reform strategy specifically designed for that variety?

Our answer falls somewhere between these extremes. While we identify what we believe would be the most beneficial institutional framework for innovation and entrepreneurship, we also acknowledge that this agenda is easy to identify only at a rather high level of theoretical abstraction (Rodrik 2007), to say nothing of how difficult it may be for member states to achieve it in practice. In fact, given the many institutional complementarities in the framework conditions of member states, the idea of all of them embarking on an immediate and straightforward journey towards best-practice institutions is naïve to say the least; at worst, it may even be detrimental to achieving the very institutional reforms we advocate (Pistor 2002; Dixit 2009). Rather, a reform strategy must be tailored to each country's specific needs. Overall, the proposed institutional changes are slanted in a liberalizing direction, but this does not mean that one-size-fits-all policy reforms towards freer markets are likely to be successful, at least not immediately. Below, we identify several points to which such a strategy should adhere.

First, a European reform agenda, even though its eyes should be set on liberalization, needs sophistication. While the identification of best-practice institutions is a *sine qua non* for the agenda to be successful, it must be accompanied by a recognition that first-order economic principles—the protection of property, contract enforcement, market competition, etc.—do not map onto unique policy packages. Hence, no unique correspondence exists between functionally good institutions and the form that such institutions take. Desirable economic ends can be achieved through a number of different institutional bundles. What is most appropriate is highly context-dependent; at worst, a thoughtless introduction of first-class legal institutions can backfire if instead of taking hold they undermine existing domestic institutions (Rodrik 2008). It falls on reformers to creatively package the principles into institutional designs that are sensitive to local constraints and take advantage of local opportunities.

Second, a reform agenda must be appropriately concrete. Most historical and econometric studies about institutions and growth (e.g., North and Thomas 1973; Hall and Jones 1999; Acemoglu et al. 2001) tend to remain at a high level of generality and do not provide much policy guidance (Besley and Burgess 2003; Rodrik 2008). In this study, we have attempted to go beyond abstract reasoning and drilled down to the specific effects of particular measures. Much more work is required in this respect, but hopefully, we have proceeded somewhat further down the ladder of concreteness.

Third, the reform agenda must prioritize, and the EOE and VoC perspectives are valuable for understanding how. The EOE perspective helps us identify which institutions matter the most for the key actors in the entrepreneurial ecosystem, whereas the VoC perspective elucidates how countries group with respect to these institutions and hints at the institutional complementarities that characterize a particular cluster of countries. Much more work is required here, an important part of which is to identify and remove so-called institutional bottlenecks (Acs et al. 2014). Doing so will make it possible to more directly identify the problems that ought to be the top priority within a cluster. Furthermore, countries in a cluster can be more or less successful, and their relative rank within the cluster has important informational and practical value when the reform process is undertaken. Rather than trying to leap-frog directly to an institutional bliss point, a laggard within a cluster should try to become more like the leader in its cluster in the short and medium term. This goal is likely to be more attainable by virtue of its relative modesty and because the reforming country then aspires to something that has been tried by a country with a similar institutional setup.

Lastly, it is important that the reform process is incremental and leaves room for experimentation rather than imitation without reflection. From a Schumpeterian perspective, the quest to develop an optimal set of legal rules ignores a central feature of successful economic development, namely, the continuous change, innovation and adaptation of institutions and organizations in a competitive environment. Reforms that are tailor-made to a country's specific constraints and opportunities through experimentation during a discovery process will likely be more beneficial than reforms based on mere imitation (Lau et al. 2000; Qian 2002; Hausmann and Rodrik 2003; Imbs and Wacziarg 2003; Sabel and Reddy 2007). That being said, given the complexities involved, it is important to keep in mind that simple legal principles often are preferable to a detail-oriented case-by-case approach. One possibility is to strive for the sort of "simple rules for a complex world" advocated by Epstein (2009).

We have proposed institutional reforms pertaining to nine broad areas:

(i) *The rule of law and protection of property rights.* These are the most fundamental rules of the game, and all member states must ensure that they are stable and secure. Regarding intellectual property rights, an important balance must be struck. The rules must be strong enough to incentivize investments in innovation, yet weak enough to allow knowledge diffusion.

(ii) *Taxation.* Many types of taxes affect entrepreneurial decisions. While tax rates should generally be low or moderate, policy makers should strive for simplicity rather than (targeted) exceptions and for a high degree of tax neutrality across owner categories, sources of finance, and different types of economic activities.

(iii) *Savings, capital and finance.* These institutions should be reformed to support more private wealth formation and the creation of a dynamic venture capital industry, as these are crucial sources of finance, particularly in the early stages of an entrepreneurial project. As a large share of savings in the economy currently goes into pension funds, it is important that at least part of these assets can also be invested in entrepreneurial firms, not just in real estate, public stock and bonds.

(iv) *Labor markets and social security.* Institutions should facilitate the recruitment of workers with the necessary competencies, and reforms should strive for the removal of legal and institutional hurdles. Overly stringent employment regulations may also create strong incentives for actors in the skill structure to devise arrangements to circumvent the regulations, including the emergence of an underground economy. Furthermore, incentives are best served by government income insurance systems that encourage activation, mobility and risk-taking. Social security institutions should enable the portability of tenure rights and pension plans, as well as a full decoupling of health insurance from the current employer to avoid punishing those individuals who leave a tenured job to realize entrepreneurial ideas.

(v) *Regulation of goods and service markets.* Preventing market-leading incumbents from unduly exploiting their dominant market position is essential. Lowered entry barriers are key to this reform area, as is the opening of areas that are typically closed to private production, such as healthcare and schooling. Within a well-designed system of public financing, sizeable private production and contestability should be encouraged.

(vi) *Bankruptcy law and insolvency regulation.* Entrepreneurial failure provides valuable information to other economic actors. Such ventures must be discontinued so that their resources can be redirected to more productive uses. Bankruptcy law and insolvency regulation should therefore be relatively generous and allow for a "second chance". However, it should not be too easy to file for bankruptcy, as that would encourage exploitation and destructive entrepreneurship, harming creditors as well as the rest of the community.

(vii) *R&D, commercialization and knowledge spillovers.* R&D-spending is an input; for it to translate into economic growth, entrepreneurs must exploit the inventions by introducing new methods of production or new products in the marketplace. Hence, instead of focusing on quantitative spending goals and targeted R&D support, policy should strive to generally make it easier to start and grow businesses.

(viii) *Incentives for human capital investment.* Policy should strive to create incentives that encourage the individual to acquire knowledge and skills whether through formal or workplace education. There must also be incentives to supply such opportunities by the education system itself. In particular, the U.S. university system could be a role model in that it seems more responsive to the economic needs of society than European university systems, although Europe must avoid the steep tuition fees that would hinder talented students from entering the university.

(ix) *Informal institutions.* Informal institutions affect the workings of formal institutions but may also be important for the fostering of entrepreneurship in its own right. The social legitimacy of entrepreneurs is particularly important in this respect. Likewise, norms and habits that facilitate cooperation and impersonal exchange need to be strengthened, especially with respect to trust. High-trust environments have been found to nurture market entry, enterprise growth and productive entrepreneurship. However, the extent to which policy can influence this is unclear. Furthermore, informal institutions vary considerably across regions, which is likely to affect the level at which measures should be implemented.

In summary, we hope that this work has inspired both confidence and humility regarding Europe's innovation future. Later work could analyze and present specific policy proposals linked to the different clusters of European countries in more detail. A good starting point for a more detailed reform agenda would be to identify the leader in each cluster and base reform advice directed to that cluster or the individual countries matching the leader's institutional framework.

References

Acemoglu, D., Johnson, S., & Robinson, J. A. (2001). The colonial origins of comparative development: An empirical investigation. *American Economic Review, 91*(5), 1369–1401.

Acs, Z. J., Autio, E., & Szerb, L. (2014). *Global entrepreneurship and development index 2014*. Washington, D.C.: Global Entrepreneurship and Development Institute.

Besley, T., & Burgess, R. (2003). Halving global poverty. *Journal of Economic Perspectives, 17* (3), 3–22.

Dixit, A. K. (2009). Governance, institutions and economic activity. *American Economic Review, 99*(1), 3–24.

Epstein, R. A. (2009). *Simple rules for a complex world*. Cambridge, MA: Harvard University Press.

Hall, R. E., & Jones, C. I. (1999). Why do some countries produce so much more output per worker than others? *Quarterly Journal of Economics, 114*(1), 83–116.

Hausmann, R., & Rodrik, D. (2003). Economic development as self-discovery. *Journal of Development Economics, 72*(2), 603–633.

Imbs, J., & Wacziarg, R. (2003). Stages of diversification. *American Economic Review, 93*(1), 63–86.

Lau, L. J., Qian, Y., & Roland, G. (2000). Reform without losers: An interpretation of China's dual track approach to transition. *Journal of Political Economy, 108*(1), 120–143.

North, D. C., & Thomas, R. P. (1973). *The rise of the Western World: A new economic history*. New York: Cambridge University Press.

Pistor, K. (2002). The standardization of law and its effect on developing economies. *American Journal of Comparative Law, 50*(1), 97–130.

Qian, Y. (2002). How reform worked in China. William Davidson Institute Working Paper No. 473. Ann Arbor, MI: William Davidson Institute.

Rodrik, D. (2007). *One economics, many recipes: Globalization, institutions, and economic growth*. Princeton, NJ and Oxford: Princeton University Press.

Rodrik, D. (2008). Second-best institutions. *American Economic Review, 98*(2), 100–104.

Sabel, C. F., & Reddy, S. (2007). Learning to learn: Undoing the Gordian knot of development today. *Challenge, 50*(5), 73–92.

Appendix

See Figs. A.1, A.2, A.3, A.4, A.5, A.6 and Tables A.1, A.2, A.3, A.4.

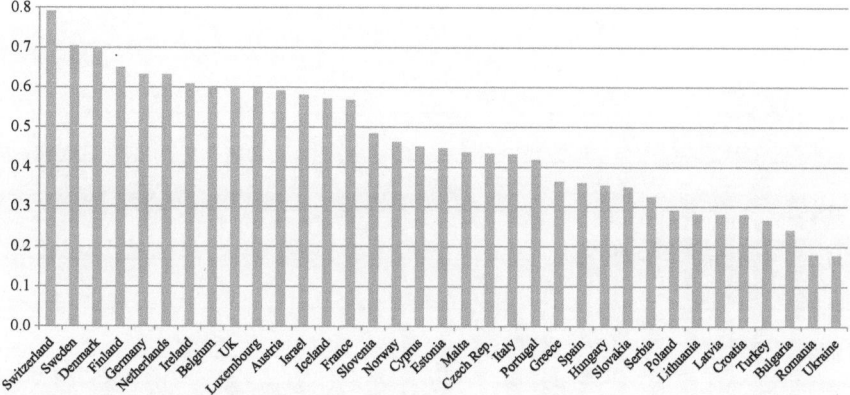

Fig. A.1 Innovation score of EU member countries and other rich European countries, 2015. *Note* The index is a composite of a total of 25 different indicators. *Source* European Union (2016)

N. Elert et al., *Institutional Reform for Innovation and Entrepreneurship*,
SpringerBriefs in Economics, DOI 10.1007/978-3-319-55092-3

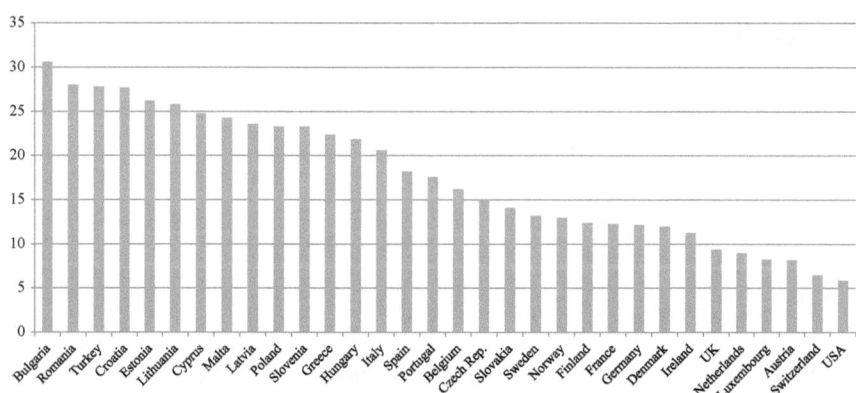

Fig. A.2 The size of the shadow economy in European countries and the U.S. in 2015 (in % of official GDP). *Source* Schneider (2015)

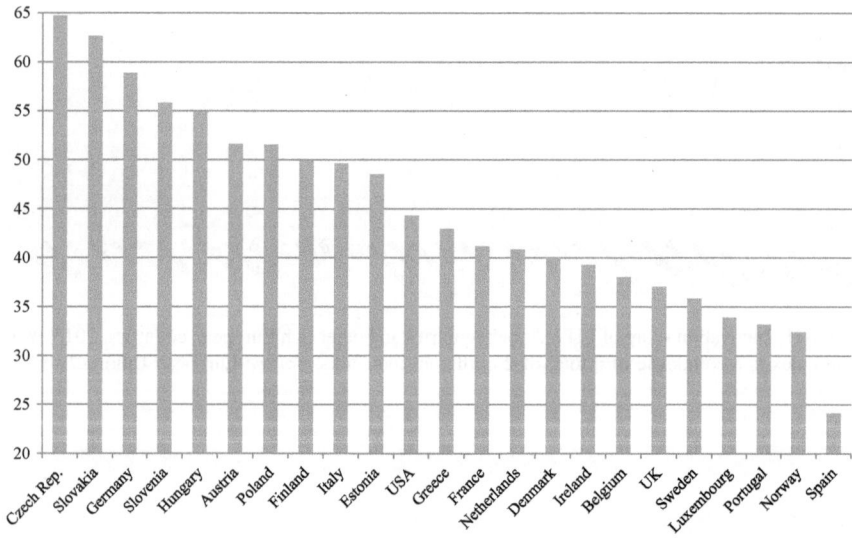

Fig. A.3 Share of 25–34 year olds with upper secondary or post-secondary non-tertiary education in EU countries and the U.S., 2014. *Source* OECD (2016)

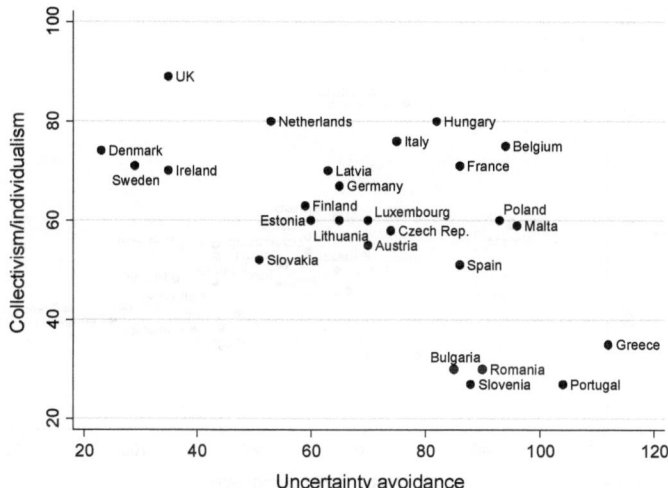

Fig. A.4 Collectivism/individualism and uncertainty avoidance in EU countries. *Note* Collectivism/individualism describes a society's preference for collectivism versus individualism. The high side (individualism) describes a preference for a loosely-knit social framework in which individuals are expected to take care of only themselves and their immediate families, whereas the low side (collectivism) represents a preference for a tightly-knit framework in society in which individuals can expect their relatives or members of a particular in-group to look after them in exchange for unquestioning loyalty. Uncertainty avoidance expresses the degree to which the members of a society feel uncomfortable with uncertainty and ambiguity about the future; high-scoring countries maintain rigid codes of belief and behavior and are intolerant of unorthodox behavior and ideas, whereas low scoring countries maintain a more relaxed attitude in which practice counts more than principles. *Source* Hofstede (2010), "Dimension Data Matrix", http://www.geerthofstede.nl/dimension-data-matrix

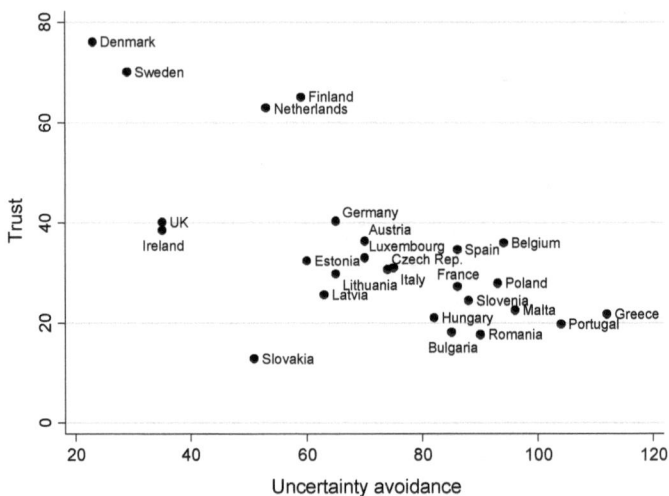

Fig. A.5 Trust and uncertainty avoidance in EU countries. *Note* Trust is measured as the share of people in a country who believe that most people can be trusted. Uncertainty avoidance expresses the degree to which the members of a society feel uncomfortable with uncertainty and ambiguity about the future; high-scoring countries maintain rigid codes of belief and behavior and are intolerant of unorthodox behavior and ideas, whereas low scoring countries maintain a more relaxed attitude in which practice counts more than principles. *Source* European Value Survey 2008 and Hofstede (2010), "Dimension Data Matrix", http://www.geerthofstede.nl/dimension-data-matrix

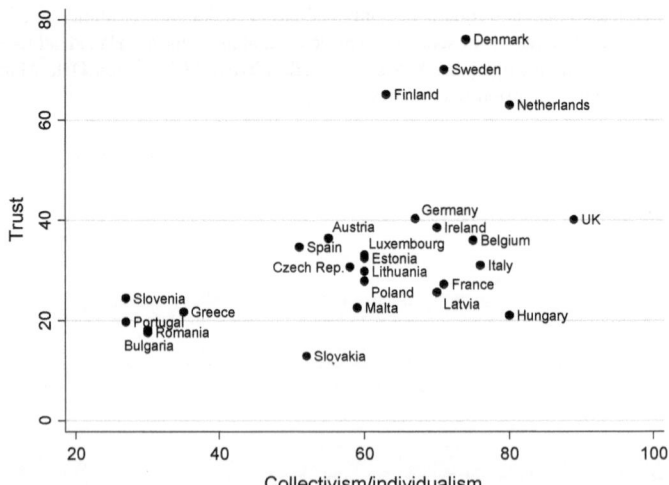

Fig. A.6 Trust and collectivism/individualism in EU countries. *Note* Trust is measured as the share of people in a country who believe that most people can be trusted. Collectivism/individualism describes a society's preference for collectivism versus individualism. The high side (individualism) describes a preference for a loosely-knit social framework in which individuals are expected to take care of only themselves and their immediate families, whereas the low side (collectivism) represents a preference for a tightly-knit framework in society in which individuals can expect their relatives or members of a particular in-group to look after them in exchange for unquestioning loyalty. *Source* European Value Survey 2008 and Hofstede (2010), "Dimension Data Matrix", http://www.geerthofstede.nl/dimension-data-matrix

Table A.1 The standard dividend and capital gains tax rate in EU member countries and the U.S., 2012

Country	Dividends	Capital gains
Austria	25.0	25.0
Belgium	25.0	0.0
Bulgaria	5.0	10.0
Croatia	n/a	n/a
Cyprus	20.0	0.0
Czech Republic	15.0	0.0
Denmark	42.0	42.0
Estonia	0.0	21.0
Finland	22.4	32.0
France	41.1	32.5
Germany	26.4	25.0
Greece	25.0	0.0
Hungary	16.0	16.0
Ireland	41.0	30.0
Italy	20.0	20.0
Latvia	10.0	15.0
Lithuania	20.0	0.0
Luxembourg	19.5	0.0
Malta	0.0	35.0
Netherlands	25.0	0.0
Poland	19.0	19.0
Portugal	25.0	25.0
Romania	16.0	16.0
Slovakia	0.0	19.0
Slovenia	20.0	0.0
Spain	27.0	27.0
Sweden	30.0	30.0
UK	36.1	28.0
USA	19.0	19.1

Source Carroll et al. (2012)

Table A.2 Direct government funding of business R&D and tax incentives for R&D, percentage of GDP 2013

Country	Direct funding	Indirect support (through R&D tax incentives)	Direct and indirect funding	Government funding as % of total BERD
Austria	0.15	0.12	0.27	12.8
Belgium (2012)	0.10	0.20	0.30	17.0
Czech Republic	0.12	0.06	0.18	16.1
Denmark	0.06	0.06	0.12	6.1
Estonia	0.08	0.00	0.08	12.9
Finland	0.06	0.01	0.07	3.3
France	0.11	0.26	0.37	25.3
Germany	0.08	0.00	0.08	4.0
Greece	0.02	0.04	0.06	21.4
Hungary	0.19	0.13	0.32	32.7
Ireland (2012)	0.07	0.16	0.23	20.7
Italy	0.05	0.00	0.05	6.9
Netherlands	0.02	0.15	0.17	15.3
Poland	0.04	–	0.04	9.1
Portugal	0.04	0.09	0.13	22.0
Slovakia	0.02	0.00	0.02	6.1
Slovenia	0.25	0.09	0.34	18.4
Spain (2012)	0.08	0.02	0.10	15.6
Sweden	0.14	0.00	0.14	6.6
UK	0.08	0.08	0.16	14.5
USA (2012)	0.19	0.07	0.26	13.5

Source OECD Science, Technology and Industry Scoreboard 2015

Table A.3 State of cluster development in EU countries and the U.S., 2015

Country	Value	Score (0–100)
USA	5.49	74.8
Germany	5.46	74.4
Italy	5.46	74.3
UK	5.30	71.7
Netherlands	5.22	70.3
Luxembourg	5.07	67.8
Austria	4.93	65.4
Finland	4.91	65.1
Ireland	4.89	64.8
Sweden	4.82	63.7
Belgium	4.58	59.6
Denmark	4.46	57.7
France	4.46	57.7
Portugal	4.16	52.6
Malta	3.96	49.3
Spain	3.92	48.7
Cyprus	3.89	48.2
Czech Republic	3.88	48.1
Slovakia	3.88	48.0
Estonia	3.76	45.9
Romania	3.65	44.1
Hungary	3.63	43.8
Latvia	3.60	43.3
Poland	3.58	43.0
Lithuania	3.52	41.9
Slovenia	3.46	40.9
Bulgaria	3.16	36.0
Croatia	3.05	34.2
Greece	2.95	32.5

Note Average answer to the survey question on the role of clusters in the economy: In your country, how widespread are well-developed and deep clusters (geographic concentrations of firms, suppliers, producers of related products and services, and specialized institutions in a particular field)? [1 = nonexistent; 7 = widespread in many fields]. The scores denote the distance to the frontier score of 100. *Source* World Economic Forum, Executive Opinion Survey 2014–2015, http://reports.weforum.org/global-competitiveness-report-2015-2016/

Table A.4 University/industry research collaboration in EU countries and the U.S., 2015

Country	Value	Score (0–100)
Finland	5.97	82.8
USA	5.85	80.8
United Kingdom	5.67	77.8
Belgium	5.58	76.3
Netherlands	5.38	73.0
Germany	5.34	72.3
Sweden	5.33	72.1
Ireland	5.24	70.7
Luxembourg	4.90	65.1
Denmark	4.90	65.0
Portugal	4.68	61.4
Austria	4.68	61.3
Lithuania	4.61	60.1
France	4.58	59.7
Estonia	4.36	55.9
Hungary	4.27	54.6
Cyprus	4.19	53.2
Czech Republic	4.00	50.0
Slovenia	3.96	49.3
Malta	3.86	47.6
Spain	3.77	46.2
Italy	3.73	45.5
Latvia	3.67	44.6
Romania	3.59	43.2
Poland	3.50	41.7
Croatia	3.39	39.9
Slovakia	3.36	39.3
Greece	3.06	34.4
Bulgaria	3.00	33.3

Note Average answer to the survey question: In your country, to what extent do people collaborate and share ideas between companies and universities/research institutions? [1 = not at all; 7 = to a great extent]. The score measures the distance to the leading country (=100). *Source* World Economic Forum, Executive Opinion Survey 2014–2015 (http://reports.weforum.org/global-competitiveness-report-2015–2016/)

References

Carroll, R., Pizzola, B., Hultman, E., & Segerström, M. (2012). *Corporate dividend and capital gains taxation: A comparison of Sweden to other member nations of the OECD and EU, and BRIC Countries*. Washington, DC and Stockholm: Ernst & Young.

European Union (2016). *European Innovation Scoreboard 2016*. Brussels: European Commission, Directorate-General for Internal Market, Industry, Entrepreneurship and SMEs.

OECD (2016). *OECD employment outlook 2016*. Paris: OECD.

Schneider, F. (2015). *Size and development of the shadow economy of 31 European and 5 other OECD Countries from 2003 to 2015: Different developments*. Mimeo. Linz, AUT: Department of Economics, Johannes Kepler University.

© The Author(s) 2017
N. Elert et al., *Institutional Reform for Innovation and Entrepreneurship*,
SpringerBriefs in Economics, DOI 10.1007/978-3-319-55092-3

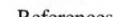